IMAGES
of America

NEW
SCOTLAND
TOWNSHIP

The Battle of Clarksville is part of a lithograph entitled *View of the Great Pass on the Helderberg Mountains*. It shows the lines of march in December 1839, derived from drawings at the time and place by T. Grenell. The sheriff and the militia are shown starting up from Clarksville to meet the angry farmers protesting the unfair demands of the VanRensselaer Patroon. (Courtesy Cherry Hill Collection.)

The "upper hotel" was located in New Salem. See page 43.

IMAGES
of America

NEW
SCOTLAND
TOWNSHIP

New Scotland Historical Association

Contributing Writers:
Robert and Marion Parmenter, Margaret Dorgan, Joseph Hogan,
Martha Slingerland, and Norma Walley

ARCADIA
PUBLISHING

Published by Arcadia Publishing
Charleston, South Carolina

Library of Congress Catalog Card Number: 00-101909

For all general information contact Arcadia Publishing at:
Telephone 843-853-2070
Fax 843-853-0044
E-Mail sales@arcadiapublishing.com
For customer service and orders:
Toll-Free 1-888-313-2665

Proceeds from this document benefit the New Scotland Historical Association.

Visit us on the Internet at www.arcadiapublishing.com

Ellen Furbeck (Houghtaling) Radliff is seated in front of her house, the first one east of Erwin's Store in New Salem. Others in the picture are her son-in-law, Albert, and her daughter, Amanda (Houghtaling) Vanderpoel. Family pictures taken in front of their homes, such as this, were common in the 1890s. Featured is the family lawnmower, a fairly new addition.

CONTENTS

This 1866 map of New Scotland, from Beers's *Atlas of Albany and Schenectady Counties*, shows the Helderbergs to the west, with the hamlets and roads as they appeared at that time. Feura Bush, Onesquethaw, Unionville, Clarksville, New Salem, and New Scotland were all substantial settlements. Voorheesville did not exist at the time but is now located where the railroad tracks cross in the northern part of the town.

INTRODUCTION

One of the most difficult things for each generation to pass down to succeeding generations is what we look like. Oral histories and the evaluation of the written word have provided endless volumes of information. Art forms have evolved over the ages through drawing, painting, sculpting, and other methods. Each of these gives some idea of how people in the past may have looked. It was not, however, until the mid-19th-century invention of photography that we could see exactly how people and communities looked from that time on. The photographs contained in *New Scotland Township* illustrate the development of the communities in the town from 1860 to 1980. These photographs came from a variety of sources. The majority of them came from existing collections, but many were collected specifically for this publication.

The earliest European settlement of the area now known as New Scotland occurred in the early 17th century. In 1629, a patroonship was granted to Killian VanRensselaer by the Dutch West India Company. This patroonship would prove to be a strong and lasting economic and political influence in the area until the mid-19th century. The end of the patroon's claim on the area came about as a result of the famous Anti-Rent Wars and the legislation that followed.

By the 18th century, many settlers from Holland, Scotland, England, and elsewhere began to populate the choicest land for farmsteads. After the American Revolution, the population began to grow significantly. Various church congregations (Dutch Reformed, Presbyterian, Methodist, and others) were formed and churches were erected in the growing hamlets. The church structures not only provided for the religious needs of the people, but also served as meeting halls and social centers. By the early 19th century, schools were being established in each of the hamlets. The result of this would be the development of real communities throughout the future town's area.

On April 25, 1832, the Town of New Scotland was created by an act of the state legislature. All of the town's previous jurisdiction had formerly been part of the Town of Bethlehem.

The early economy of the area was primarily based on agriculture. Food crops and fodder for the livestock were raised. Hops were harvested extensively for shipment to nearby breweries in the city of Albany. Apples, plums, and other fruits were later added to this list of valuable produce. Many still-existing farms date back to this early period.

After the Civil War, the Town of New Scotland, along with the rest of the nation, began to feel the influence of improved communication and transportation brought about by the new technology of the day. Perhaps the single greatest impact on the town was the establishment of the railroad, which allowed farms to serve a much larger market than before. Mercantile and industrial activity was possible in an ever-increasing and diversified level. This rapid expansion of economic activity would have a profound effect on community development and demographic growth within the town.

Today, the Town of New Scotland consists of a total area of 58 square miles. Its population has grown from 2,030 in 1835 to nearly 10,000 people in the last few years. The villages and hamlets of the town include Clarksville, Feura Bush, New Salem, New Scotland, Onesquethaw (Tarrytown), Unionville, and Voorheesville.

Clarksville is located in the southwestern part of the town. It was first settled in the late 18th century and was originally referred to as West Bethlehem. The present name came from Adam A. Clark, a prominent resident who settled there by 1822. At one time, Clarksville was the largest community in the town, with several hotels and many businesses.

Feura Bush, previously referred to as Moakville and later Jerusalem, is a small hamlet in the southeastern part of the town. It once had a station for the West Shore Railroad. The name change came about with the establishment of the post office because too many hamlets in the state were called Jerusalem. The name of Feura Bush, meaning "fire bush," was chosen because sunlight reflecting off the pine trees made the hills appear to be on fire.

New Salem, which was settled as early as 1770, is located slightly northwest of the center of New Scotland. It was originally called Punkintown, a name which is said to have originated from a legend. According to the story, a sow and her litter were able to live inside a "punkin," because the "punkins" grown here were so large. However, when the post office arrived, the name was changed to New Salem.

The hamlet of New Scotland is located east of New Salem. It was settled as early as 1765 by many Scotch settlers, hence the name. The West Shore Railroad established a line running through the hamlet in 1865, with a station in the hamlet. New Scotland's most famous farm product was the "Bender Melon," produced on the Charles Bender Farm. Much hay was also shipped from here. The first town meeting was held here in 1833.

The hamlet of Onesquethaw is located nearly two miles southeast of Clarksville. Onesquethaw is known locally as Tarrytown. According to legend, a large structure called the "castle" had a bar-room where patrons would "tarry" until all hours. The building is long gone, but the name remains. The Onesquethaw Creek flows near this area. Stone was quarried here when the Erie Canal was under construction. Some of the oldest homes in the town (many of them stone) can be found in the Onesquethaw area, which is a Historic District.

Unionville, a small hamlet, is in the eastern part of the town north of Feura Bush. Some members of the Jerusalem and Salem Churches united to form Union Church in 1824. The hamlet—with a hotel, school, blacksmith shops, and homes—soon followed. To avoid confusion over identity with another community, the post office was called Union Church.

The village of Voorheesville, incorporated in 1899, is located in the northern part of the town. It is New Scotland's largest, youngest and only incorporated village. Its existence and economic importance was established by the junction of two railroad lines (the Albany & Susquehanna and West Shore Railroads) in the 1860s. The railroad was soon followed by the establishment of hotels, stores, and industries. The name Voorheesville is taken from Alonzo B. Voorhees, a lawyer from Albany. Apparently, when he applied for a post office for the village, he wrote in the name "Voorheesville." The name would change one additional time. From August 1890 to August 1892 the village became known as Farlin, named after Dudley Farlin, a career railroad agent. However, the village and post office went back to being called Voorheesville and has remained so ever since.

The six chapters of *New Scotland Township* cover people, homes, community scenes, schools, churches, occupations, recreation, and transportation. As a general rule, we begin each chapter in the southernmost part of the town and move to the north. Many of the pictures in this collection contain an amazing amount of detail no matter what the subject. Look closely as you make your way through the chapters.

—Robert Parmenter, Town Historian

One

HOMES AND CITIZENS

This is the Edmund Raynsford Home as it looked in the 1880s. Located on the corner of the Plank Road and North Road (Routes 85 and 85A) in New Scotland, this saltbox-style building dates to the early 1800s. In the late 1880s, the house burned. The first town meeting is thought to have been held in this home on April 9, 1833. Raynsford was the New Scotland postmaster (1824–1845) and owned and operated the hotel across the road for many years. He was the commissioner of schools, a teacher, and later a member of the state assembly. The picket fence, common in many hamlets, extended down both sides of the road, well past the church. This chapter features many early New Scotland families and their homes.

A busy lady
WITH HER BROADCASTING
"Save the Baby"
AND
POULTRY CONSULTANT WORK

Sincerely yours,
MRS. ALICE A. ROBERTS
POULTRY CONSULTANT

Alice Roberts, c. 1935, was a very involved Feura Bush resident who began the Feura Bush Community Association. She held many offices in the Clarksville Grange and was a matron working with the Junior Grange. She raised bantam chickens and was a renowned judge of them at fairs around the country. She was well known for her local radio broadcasting sponsored by Save the Baby, a popular decongestant medicine.

The view across the fields toward the Selkirk Railroad yards makes a beautiful setting for the buildings on the Mathias farm on South Road near Feura Bush. The car and truck in the side yard serve to mark the era as the 1940s. Katherine Mathias can be seen standing next to the car. The barns in the distance, part of the former Onion farm (later Becker), is where the General Electric office complex is presently located.

The Slingerland-Parks house on Route 32 (Indian Fields Road) was built in 1762 by Teunis Slingerland (1723–1800). Slingerland was the grandson of Teunis Cornelis Slingerland, who with his son-in-law, bought a large tract of land from the Native Americans in 1685. The original front entrance, facing the Onesquethaw Creek, cannot be seen in this 1952 picture.

This home on Rowe Road (along the Onesquethaw Creek) was built by Solomon Rowe c. 1890. It was a productive farm when the Ira Vanderbilts occupied the house. A succession of owners have helped to preserve the integrity of the house. The lattice around the roof line has playing card emblems. The story goes that the builder was a gambler and used all the card figures except the diamonds, indicating that he had buried diamonds somewhere in the house. This picture dates to 1949.

This old stone home on the Onesquethaw Creek Road was built in 1756 by Gerrit VanZandt on land purchased from Stephen VanRensselaer. It was partially fortified during the French and Indian War with bars on the lower windows. The top floor served as a barracks for British troops garrisoned there. The windows and doors are original. A free-standing building to the rear is thought to have been a kitchen. This picture dates to 1949.

This is an interior view of the Johannes Appel–Hans Slingerland house as it appeared c. 1960. Located on Dryden Lane, off the Onesquethaw Creek Road, it is one of the earliest houses in the town, built c. 1700. Notice the original paneling and hinges on the large cupboards to the left of the fireplace. At the time the photograph was taken, it was the home of Mr. and Mrs. Daniel P. Dryden.

Pvt. William H. Hopkins was the son of Clarence and Ella Hopkins of Unionville. He was drafted into the U.S. Army at Camp Devens, Massachusetts, in September 1917. He went overseas in April 1918 and served with the expeditionary forces in France. His daughter, Dorothy Wilkenson, reported that "he went 'over the top' seven times and once was under fire for 27 days, yet he never received a scratch."

This 1952 picture shows the DeLong-Vanderbilt home in Onesquethaw. It was built by the David DeLong family in 1807, and the land has been farmed continuously since that time. This Dutch-style stone house with spacious fireplaces and hand-hewn beams is set in the beautiful countryside of corn and hay fields. The present owners are David and Mary Ellen (Vanderbilt) Domblewski. Mary Ellen is a descendent of David DeLong's daughter, Abiah, and her husband, Garrett Vanderbilt.

Bertha Jane Vanderbilt was born on June 18, 1884 in the Vanderbilt homestead (see page 13) in what was then called Tarrytown. She was the oldest child of Gulian and Alice Brougham Vanderbilt. Bertha later attended the one-room schoolhouse (see page 85) that was located near the Onesquethaw Reformed church across the road from her home. Her niece is pictured in front of her family's stone home in 1886, wearing clothes typical of the time.

Bertha Vanderbilt grew up and married Bennett Beck. Bertha was an active member in the Onesquethaw Reformed Church throughout her life and was honored for being the oldest member of the congregation in 1974. Here she is pictured in front of the church, probably in the early 1960s. She returned to the home of her brother Leroy (the Vanderbilt home) during her final years. She died in the home where she was born on December 6, 1975.

Pictured here is a lovely stone house on Nine Mile Lane that was built before 1800. For many years, this was a VanAtten farm. In his will of 1866, Benjamin VanAtten refers to it as "the Winne place." It is now owned by Michael Rice. Nine Mile Lane gets its name from the nine mile-marker (from Albany) that is located where it intersects with Delaware Turnpike. It once connected with Brownrigg Road.

This house was built in 1855 by Anthony and Ann Slingerland on Delaware Turnpike near Unionville. It sheltered four generations of the Slingerland family before it was destroyed by fire on July 2, 1947. The house that was built on the same foundation later that year is now owned by James C. and Jackie Slingerland, whose children are the sixth generation on this site. This photograph dates to 1940.

This 1891 photograph shows the Franklin Ingraham family in front of their home on Upper Flat Rock Road, next to the Houck Neighborhood School. The house has been extensively remodeled and is now part of Tommell Farm. From left to right are Anna, Samuel, Lena, Marvin, Wallace (by the post), Walter (on the chair), Bertha, Catherine Jane McCulloch Ingraham (mother), Franklin Ingraham (father), and Fred.

John VanDerHeyden Bradt bought this house, located just below the Unionville Hotel, in 1867. After his death in 1905, his adopted daughter, Lillie, and her husband inherited the house and made extensive changes. The people in the photograph are, from left to right, as follows: DeWitt VanderZee, Myron Scarlet, Mr. Bradt, Rev. John Scarlett, Mrs. Scarlett, and Lillie Bradt VanderZee, whose husband, Cornelius, was taking the picture.

16

This is a photograph of Bertha Ingraham as a teenager. She was born on April 21, 1886, the seventh child of Franklin and Catherine Jane McCulloch Ingraham. Her father's grandfather, Samuel Ingraham, was keeping a tavern in Clarksville by 1800. Her maternal grandmother was Mariah Slingerland McCulloch, who was called one of the "mill girls" because her father ran the Slingerland Mill on Route 32.

This 1971 photograph shows Bertha Ingraham Slingerland at age 85. She married Amasa Slingerland on October 7, 1907, and had two children: Dorothy Agnes, who was born on February 3, 1911, and Harold Amasa, who took this picture and was born on February 28, 1915. Her husband, a farmer, was also the supervisor for the Town of New Scotland from 1931 to 1947. He died on April 27, 1966. Bertha lived until July 31, 1974.

Mr. and Mrs. Adam Clark are shown c. 1845. He was born in Westerly, Rhode Island, in 1792 and served in the War of 1812. He came to "West Bethlehem" in 1822 and ran a hotel there. He became postmaster in 1826. When the Town of New Scotland formed in 1832, the post office's name was changed to Clarksville in his honor. He and his wife, Betsey Wood, had no children but adopted Mary Blodgett. He died in 1856.

Twins Ella and Vera and their brother, Earl Ingraham, with their grandmother, Ellen Flansburg-VanDerZee-Hendrickson, pose on the north side of Delaware Turnpike in Clarksville c. 1910. Notice the Central Hotel, with columns on the porch, in the center of the photograph. To the right is the triangle building. The children's father, Gus Ingraham, owned and operated a blacksmith shop in Clarksville.

Harriet Flansburg O'Brien was born on November 9, 1855. She was the daughter of Michael and Catherine Simmons Flansburg of Clarksville. She married Smith O'Brien on August 18, 1878 and had two daughters: Grace, who was born on May 20, 1879, and Mabel, who was born on March 31, 1886. Harriet's diary for 1895 survives, presenting a picture of life in Clarksville. After her death, her husband moved to Albany.

The Honorable Smith O'Brien poses with his daughter, Mabel, c. 1905. He was born in Berne on February 12, 1850. In 1875, he began to work in the law office of Barret H. Staats of Clarksville. He graduated from Albany Law School in 1878 and was married that year to Harriet Flansburg. He practiced law in Clarksville and Albany and was elected to the state assembly in 1885. Mabel married Everett Hallenbeck and resided near Voorheesville.

19

Thomas Relyea of Clarksville, seen here *c.* 1865, was a private in the 82nd Regiment Infantry National Guard for the state of New York. He enrolled for a seven-year enlistment on May 1, 1865, at the end of the Civil War. The end of the war shortened his enlistment. He was discharged from the active militia of New York on August 29, 1868 because his regiment was disbanded under orders of the commander in chief.

Bill Chattin and Marilyn Chattin Adriance of Clarksville posed for this picture *c.* 1964. Bill restored this 1913 Model T Ford with a maroon body, black fenders, and brass trim, in his garage at "Chattin's Hoe Down Corners." In addition to his interest in restoring old cars, Bill was well known for teaching and calling square dances throughout the town for many years.

Martin Spring, seen here c. 1930, was really a pond that reportedly was located three houses east of the Reformed church in New Salem. The pond is now gone but the house remains. Water from the mountain, near the present-day Town Highway Department Barns, flowed downhill and was stored here before being pumped to Slingerlands. Claude Hotaling was the first water superintendent in 1928.

The farmhouse shown in this c. 1880 photograph was the home of the Albert Winne family on Old Road in New Salem. It was built around 1865 by Albert's father, John Winne. The people in the photograph are not identified but are almost certainly members of the Winne family. For the past 40 years, this has been the home of John and Sue Livingston. Sue is a descendent of the Winne family.

This c. 1870 photograph shows Fannie Moak Allen, the wife of David J. Allen. She was born on August 19, 1812 to Joseph and Harriet Taylor Moak and was the granddaughter of Jacob Moak of New Scotland. She grew up on the Moak homestead on Clipp Road. She and David married on May 24, 1834 and had nine children. She died on March 21, 1903.

This serious-looking man is David J. Allen, the husband of Fannie and son of John and Nancy McCulloch Allen. He was born on January 6, 1806 in the Allen homestead on Clipp Road. When he was 22 years old, his grandfather sent him to deliver a letter to the Patroon's agent. In the letter, he stated that young David was "as steady and industrious young lad as there was in the town." He ran the family farm on Clipp Road until his death in 1876.

This is the David Allen house on Clipp Road c. 1945, now owned by Ellie Haase. The original stone portion on the left dates to 1779. Here, after a snowstorm, we can see a frame section added on an angle. A later addition has since been built, filling in the angle between the two structures. This shows a lovely view of Wolf Hill across the valley, which is now the location of the Vly Creek Reservoir.

The Bullock-Hurst home is seen here in 1974. The stone portion was built by John Bullock and his slaves in 1787. The brick portion was added in the 19th century. John's son, Matthew, inherited the homestead in 1802. He became well known for the short-horned cattle, which he introduced in 1815 and continued to breed and improve. The Hurst family bought the property after the Civil War and owned it for many years.

This is the Whitbeck home in New Scotland as it looked in 1897. Jay M. Whitbeck, standing in the wagon, sold Page Woven Wire Fence, as the horse advertises. You can see some of this fence to the left of the house. Note the outbuildings and, under the horse, Jay's prize rooster. Standing on the porch is Jay's wife, Henrietta. The child to the right of the horse is their daughter, Pauline. This home still stands on what is now Whitbeck Lane, parallel to Route 85, near the railroad overpass.

This late-19th-century photograph shows Pine Knoll as it originally appeared. It is located on the corner of Bullock and New Scotland Roads in New Scotland. It was built by Aaron Hotaling around 1850, with several additions made over the years by the Hotaling family. In 1923, Harris Hotaling sold it to the famous writer and historian Arthur Pound. Mr. Pound made additional architectural changes, giving the house its present appearance.

In the front seat sit Charles Bender and Gladys Schell while Mrs. TenEyck and Mrs. Charles Bender sit in the back seat of Mr. Bender's Maxwell. Here, the group arrives at the Bender home in New Scotland c. 1920. Michael Forrester is sitting on the lawn. In the 1880s, Mr. Bender began developing a variety of cantaloupe which was to become known as the famous Bender Melon.

The man in this *c.* 1905 photograph, Peter Hart, was a hired hand on an area Crounse farm. According to an article by local historian Arthur Gregg, Mr. Hart found a letter under a wood pile. The letter, dated September 1885, reportedly disclosed the location of money and gold buried in a cave in the Helderberg Escarpment. It was signed by an Englishman, John Robert Swift, who wrote that he had killed his partner in crime and was about to take his own life. He left instructions for the letter to be printed in the *Albany Journal* and to send a copy to Park Place in London, England, so that his friends would know what had happened to him. This is a wonderful story, but the treasure has never been found. Mr. Hart supposedly had the map that was mentioned in the letter, and many people searched for the cave.

This was the home of Edna (Wynkoop) and Myndert Crounse on Route 85A in Voorheesville. Myndert moved here in 1911. While the house was new, the barns were over 50 years old at the time. Today, behind the barn, you can still see a small saltbox structure which was the original home when it was a tenant farm. It originally stood next to the stream. The large barn on the left burned in the early 1950s. Myndert had a large apple orchard and also sold milk.

This home on New Salem Road currently belongs to the Richard Frohlich family. It was purchased in 1909 by his grandparents, Everett and Mabel (O'Brien) Hallenbeck. The one-story portion on the right was the original home built by W. McMillen in the early 1800s. The middle portion was the first addition. The second addition on the left dates to 1862. The present Route 85A was a dirt road when this photograph was taken in 1920.

The Reverend and Mrs. S.B. Gregg pose with their children, Arthur and Jenny, in 1898. Reverend Gregg was the minister at the Voorheesville Methodist Church from 1897 to 1899. When Arthur grew up, he became a noted author, journalist, and local historian. Many of the numerous articles that he wrote for the *Altamont Enterprise* were published in his book *Old Hellebergh*.

Alice, Lena, and Bessie VanAuken pose on the front lawn of their Valley View Farm on Crow Ridge Road *c.* 1905. Alice became a milliner, Lena became a teacher, and Bessie became a dressmaker. They had two brothers, one of whom became a doctor and the other a farmer. This serves to illustrate some of the career choices available at the turn of the century. This is currently the home of Mark Baumbach.

Two

COMMUNITY SCENES

The view of the Helderberg Mountains and New Salem from the Mount Pleasant Cemetery, c. 1900, looks much different today. One can see Plank Road (Route 85) in the center and the New Salem Reformed church further down the road. The top of the mountain, as well as the foreground, looked vastly different with acres of cleared fields. The entire escarpment is clearly visible. Hedgerows are clearly defined. Where once was farmland, today is mostly brush, young forest, and many more homes. Perhaps this man enjoyed a picnic at the cemetery, a popular outing at the time. Community scenes in and around all the hamlets are noticeably changed from what they were in the past.

The Feura Bush Hotel is shown as it appeared from the church lawn *c.* 1925. Note the car, bicycle, and carriage sheds, all of which denote the various modes of transportation at the time. The hotel was built in the early 19th century. Workers stayed here when quarrying rock for the Erie Canal. Lewis Rothaupt operated the business when Feura Bush was still called Jerusalem, prior to 1912. In addition to a hotel, the building has housed a roller-skating rink and post office. Currently, it has apartments in it.

The Rothaupt family is posing in front of their home on Main Street in Feura Bush *c.* 1890. The home still stands today. Three children known to be in the picture are Dave, Dewey, and their sister, Rose. Lewis Rothaupt first operated a blacksmith shop, which later became an automotive garage and Ford dealership operated by his sons, David and Dewey.

The Unionville Hotel, built c. 1810, is shown in 1897 when William Wemple was proprietor. At the time, the Rensselaerville-Albany Stage kept a relief team there. It contained the post office, which was called Union Church because there was already another Unionville in Orange County. Through the years, the hotel has housed various shops and a community theater group. It is now vacant and in disrepair.

On November 19, 1950, when this picture was taken, the hotel in Unionville was home to a small grocery store and ice cream shop. The owner was Mabel Degan. She lived with her husband, Albert, and their children in the east side of the building. The barn and shed—which had sheltered the stage teams and horses of guests one hundred years earlier—had been torn down earlier, leaving a two-car garage.

This peddler's wagon is on the way to its next stop in Clarksville after leaving Onesquethaw on the Tarrytown Road. The photograph was taken and developed by Maggie Flansburg Moak around noon on August 1911. The house on the left is the Scutt House and the next building beyond was the blacksmith shop. The Onesquethaw School can be seen in the background.

John T. Smith was the proprietor of the Clarksville Hotel at the time this photograph was taken in August 1911. In 1839, during the Anti-Rent Wars, this hotel was called the Clark Tavern. When the state militia arrived at Clarksville and Maj. William Bloodgood made the hotel his headquarters, it received the nickname "Fort Clark." Peddler wagons, like the one in the photograph, were a common sight throughout the town in this time period.

This is what you would see entering Clarksville from the east on Delaware Turnpike in 1912. The bell tower on the far left is the Methodist Episcopal church. To the right of the white fence, on the corner of North Road, is the foundation of the Clarksville Reformed church, which was being rebuilt after fire destroyed the original church in February of that same year.

Clarksville was a bustling hamlet at the time of this c. 1890 photograph, which shows a view looking north. The hamlet was surrounded with prosperous farms and orchards. On the left is the Clark Hotel (with an X on it). The Methodist church steeple can also be seen. The first two houses on the left burned in the fire of 1918. The long roof on the right is the carriage shed for the Empire Hotel. Several orchards can be seen in the distance.

Pictured here is the Delaware Turnpike looking east in Clarksville c. 1913. On the right, the team of horses is standing in front of Albertis VanWie's store. The post office was in the store from 1909 to 1922. The building on the left was the Clark Hotel and the next building, further east, was M.B. Earl's store.

This quiet village lane is Slingerland Avenue looking north in 1912. Today, it is paved and the trees are much bigger. James Slingerland owned the house on the right in 1890. The next house is a new house built after 1910. It was owned by Alson and Emeline Allen. James Peck owned the last house in 1890. Later, Charles VanWie, the bandmaster, lived in the house. Jesse C. Hannay operated a funeral home there until the 1960s.

The sign on the front of the old Clark Hotel, c. 1930, reads "Peter Applebee, Funeral Director." Peter started his business in the Clark House (page 59) and then moved it to the old hotel. George Ward used the building as a residence in the 1950s. Ed McNab later owned it. On February 8, 1962, the structure that was once called Fort Clark was sold to Theodore Collins of Delmar and demolished for building material.

The degree of destruction on the farm of Gilbert Brittain is very obvious in this photograph taken after a cyclone passed through on September 7, 1887. The farm was located on Wolf Hill above Clarksville. Peter Otto, a 28-year-old hired hand, was killed in one of the falling buildings. The Brittains never rebuilt, but moved to Westerlo. Gilbert (1826–1894) and his wife, Magdalene Slingerland (1826–1908), are buried in Westerlo Cemetery.

Pictured here is the aftermath of the great Clarksville fire. The fire started in Morgan Barber's hay barn at 3:30 p.m. on August 22, 1918. Most of the people of the village were attending the Methodist and Reformed Churches' annual picnic at Warners Lake. The houses in the distance (east) are along Mill Road. To the left are the houses along Delaware Turnpike. The house standing on the left belonged to Albertis VanWie.

NEW SCOTLAND, N. Y., September 16, 1918.

M *Gordon W. Miller*

PLEASE TAKE NOTICE, that the **New Scotland Mutual Insurance Company** has sustained losses to the amount of $4,915.00 by the burning of house, furniture, provisions, wearing apparel, barns, produce and farming utensils owned by the following persons, and with the following losses:

Harry Leonard $1,240, Morgan N. Barber $2,000, A. Van Wie $1,100, R. Van Wie $350, F. Dayton $225,

And that your part of the assessment to meet said losses is $ *4.04*
This assessment you are hereby requested to pay on October 19th next, at 1 P. M., to *Orville Brate*
who is duly appointed to receive the same, at the House of *C Mathias Slove* in said town.

F. VAN AUKEN, Secretary.   EDWARD HOTALING, President.

The New Scotland Mutual Association was organized on May 26, 1854. On September 26, 1859, the company reorganized and changed the name to New Scotland Mutual Insurance Company. This postcard was mailed to Gordon W. Miller of Feura Bush, indicating his liability as an investor in the company for the Clarksville Fire of August 22, 1918. Many barns, outbuildings, and at least four homes were destroyed in the fire.

This small Flatiron Building (Three Corner or Triangle Building) was located on the corner of Delaware Turnpike (Route 443) and Plank Road in Clarksville c. 1900. The point of the building faced downhill, with the base on Route 443. Sanford McNab ran a butcher shop here for many years. It was also used for offices, a store front, and various other purposes. The structure no longer exists, having been razed sometime in the 1920s.

Plank Road (now Tarrytown Road) enters the Delaware Turnpike next to the Flatiron Building c. 1900. Pictured is a roadway on both sides of the triangle building. The man is standing in front of the Central Hotel and carriage sheds. The small house with a porch is D.C. Gould's confectionery store. The building just beyond is Charles VanWie's hardware store.

This was the scene on the North Road in New Salem, facing north, c. 1905. In the foreground, a small bridge can be seen. The stream here flows under the building on the right. The barn in the center is the blacksmith shop. The Methodist church was further down the road beyond the blacksmith shop. The church closed in 1905 and the building soon became the Red Men's Hall.

The snow makes it easy to see the escarpment and large hayfield at the top of the mountain c. 1945. The fire ring, which currently hangs in front of the new firehouse, was used to summon the firemen in the event of a fire. The honor roll lists all the residents who served in World War II, with gold stars next to those who died. This corner was the original location of the Punkintown Fair.

Looking east, toward the four corners in New Salem, notice the rubble in the center—the remains of the upper hotel that burned in 1899 (see page 43). This c. 1905 photograph also shows wagons parked along the road, the New Salem Hotel, carriage sheds, the Reformed Church, Erwin's Store, and a hay wagon in front of the barn on the corner. The photograph was probably taken from near the schoolhouse.

This was J.M. Erwin's new general store in New Salem as it looked in 1902. His original store was constructed in 1875 but was destroyed by a massive fire in June 1899. Olin Sisson purchased the store and operated it for many years, also selling gasoline. The last store in this building (Mac's Superette) was operated by Ken McVee from 1950 to 1972. It has since been converted to apartments.

One of the New Salem businesses was the Helderberg Garage Towing and Wrecking Service, seen here c. 1925. With all the tourists driving from the city to Thacher Park and the hilltowns, this was a thriving business. This is the same building as shown on page 39 with a hay wagon, and on page 99 with the scouts. The windows are now larger and there are windows in the front. It is attached to the New Salem Hotel and carriage sheds.

Lambert's Store and Gas Station was on the corner in New Salem. New York State fuel tax records show this business was here in 1933. Mrs. Lambert took care of the store and sold gas, penny candy, soda, ice cream, and other groceries. Mr. Lambert picked up the milk from the dairy farms on the mountain and transported it to bottling plants in Albany. Their daughter, Helen Filkins, continued to run the store into the early 1950s.

The oxen in this photograph appear to be the same team as pictured below, although this picture was taken a few years earlier. The person to the right standing in the cart is either Luther (Stub) MacMillan or his brother Hiram MacMillan. The signs on the railing read, "Drink Orange Crush" and "Yes sir! Anndora Cigars."

Various modes of transportation appear to be looking at each other in front of the New Salem Hotel as it appeared c. 1930. Many farmers had teams of oxen to pull heavy loads such as rocks, tree stumps, and plows. Notice the Hosler's Ice Cream sign on the hotel. Standing by the chair is the hotel's owner and operator Aden Crabill with Jim Winne, John Maloney, and Wellington Winne.

This is a *c*.1910 photograph of New Salem as seen from the top of Old Road. Most impressive are the acres of orchards growing on three sides of the hamlet. The Dutch Reformed church, in the center of the picture, was the focal point of the community. This church, the fourth one to be built by this congregation, was built in 1893. The farmers who once cleared these fields would be amazed to see them covered with forests again.

On the left is Ted Kupke's New Salem garage built in 1909. It operated until 1946, when it was sold to DeWitt Carl and Dom Tork. The Carl family operated this garage at this location for many years, establishing a SAAB dealership here. The road above the house is Old Road, the original road up the mountain. In the center is the New Salem School when it had only one room.

This hotel was often referred to as the "upper hotel." It was located on the southwest corner of the intersection in New Salem. The photograph, a tintype, is believed to have been taken in the early 1880s. The steps and portion of building you see on the left is J.M. Erwin's store. Both of these buildings burned to the ground on a Saturday night in June 1899. The fire reportedly began in the store when a lamp tipped over. The hotel was the property of the Mann heirs at the time of the fire. The road between the two buildings is South Road.

The New Scotland Hotel, c. 1930, was at the intersection of Routes 85 and 85A in New Scotland. It was built c. 1830 by John Reid, and later owned by Edmund Raynsford, who lived across the road (see page 9). It served as the New Scotland post office for many years. The hotel became a popular watering hole for workers on the nearby Bender Melon Farm. Charles Bender bought the hotel, closed the bar, and turned it into three apartments.

The original Stone Well, located at the corner of Route 85 and 85A, looked much different than it does today. Herb and Dexter Davis opened the Stone Well with a delicatessen and snack bar around 1950. The Ardizones rented the building and operated an Italian-style restaurant there between c. 1954 and 1956. After this, the Davises expanded their building and had a grocery store and restaurant. The actual stone well pictured was once known for its pure water.

The Voorheesville Railroad Station, Grove Hotel, and the park in the foreground are as they appeared in 1910. The Grove Hotel was built in the 1870s by Conrad Fryer. It had 30 rooms, a dining hall, bar, and ballroom. The freight office to the right of the park is the only building still standing. Franklin E. Vosburg, the station agent, took care of the flower beds in the park.

Pictured here is downtown Voorheesville looking toward North Main Street past the railroad crossing signs. The brick house next to the Grove Hotel was built by Conrad Fryer in 1892. Fryer sponsored many enterprises here and in the outbuildings to the rear, which included a grocery store, shoemaker shop, cooper shop, blacksmith shop, butcher shop, and a livery stable, to mention a few.

The view looking up Main Street in Voorheesville, c. 1920, shows the Harris House (an early hotel) on the right. The flatiron building on the left housed the Joslin Brothers' store from 1891 to 1923. Upstairs, the Joslin brothers' wives ran a collar-making business. Notice the boardwalk extending up both sides of the muddy street.

Harriet Bell and Anna Haakes, c. 1910, pose for their father, George Bell, who took their picture in the outhouse behind their home on Maple Avenue in Voorheesville. On the left, the rear of the sanctuary of the Methodist church can be seen. The window near the peak still exists. Outhouses, which would once have been torn down, are now sold to the highest bidder as collectibles.

Gainsley's Grocery Store in Voorheesville, *c.* 1925, was in the same location as the former Bewsher Store. Harry Gainsley is wearing the butcher apron, with his son, Delos, next to him. The store signs read, "White House Coffee, Salada Tea, National Bread, Kellogg's PEP" and "Quick Suds."

David Haswell Wayne, *c.* 1928, stands next to his Chevrolet pick-up truck parked in the alleyway leading to his coal pocket in Voorheesville. The office is to the left. Mr. Wayne sold Blue Coal. You can see the coal pocket through the alley to the left and the Duffy-Mott Cider Mill in the distance on the other side of the tracks. This is the same alleyway as in the photograph on page 48, but nine years earlier.

This 1937 photograph shows John Hallenbeck leaving the Lasher-Pitcher Store on Main Street in Voorheesville with a box of groceries. Before it became the Lasher-Pitcher Store, it belonged to Harry Gainsley, who also ran a grocery store. The taller building to the left was the building where the first laundromat was located. All these buildings have since burned in various fires. Notice the boardwalk.

The Voorheesville Honor Roll—listing all of the Voorheesville residents who served in the armed forces during WW II—was located next to the present-day Village Hall. Many of the people whose names appear here returned to Voorheesville to live after the war. Many of them raised families there and remain to this day. The Honor Roll sign was built by Dave McCartney, the Voorheesville School shop teacher.

Three

OCCUPATIONS AND BUSINESS

The Mathias Store in Feura Bush is pictured here in 1945. It was built in the 1880s by Conrad Mathias, who operated the store for many years in the early part of the century. In later years, his wife maintained the post office there and sold penny candy. During its years as a post office, it was a popular meeting place when people picked up their mail. It was sold in 1946 and became a private home. The post office was moved to the hotel, where it was operated by Anna VanDyke. It was common in many of the hamlets for families to have grocery stores in their homes or to live upstairs over the stores. This chapter shows some of the many farms and businesses in the town, many of which no longer exist.

This creamery in Feura Bush, *c.* 1900, was operated by the Dairyman's League until 1930. It was located on Quarry Road and Route 32, next to where Houghtaling's Market is today. Area farmers delivered milk from miles around. Milk was made into buttermilk, butter, and cheese. The pig farmers in the area used what was left to feed their pigs. Herbert Lester, an experienced butter maker, was the manager beginning in 1889.

This blacksmith shop in Feura Bush, *c.* 1900, stood across from the Jerusalem church and east of the hotel. Lewis Rothaupt was the owner and operator. He later operated a blacksmith shop where the current post office is located. This building was destroyed by fire in the 1960s. Note the pile of wagon wheels on both sides of the building.

Hallenbeck's Store in Feura Bush sold groceries, flour, feed and coal. Mr. Hallenbeck is pictured here c. 1910. The store was purchased by the Vadney cousins and became Vadney Coal and Feed around WWI. Dewey Vadney later left to open his own gas station and general store across the railroad tracks. Until the 1980s, Raymond Vadney continued to sell heating oil, coal, and grain for feed. A Stewart's shop is now located on this site.

This WGY food store in Feura Bush, c. 1930, was built and operated by Edward Johnson in the 1920s and 1930s. He began by selling ice cream and groceries, but the ice cream parlor was unsuccessful. By 1930, home delivery was in demand and aided in the store's continued success. It later became an IGA market. Henry Hotaling, a brother-in-law, continued the business until his retirement in the 1950s. The building had been a restaurant since the 1970s, but today is vacant.

Threshing grain, once a common sight throughout the town, can be seen on the Amasa Slingerland farm *c.* 1940. The oats were brought from the field to the threshing machine in horse-drawn wagons. This outfit, owned by Leonard Shultes, was set up by the Slingerland barn. Harold Slingerland is bagging the grain. In the foreground is a "doodlebug," a light tractor made from an old car. During WWII, new tractors were not available.

At the Harold Slingerland farm on the Delaware Turnpike, ham and bacon were first cured in brine in the cellar of the house and then hung upstairs in the stone smokehouse. A slow fire was built in the fireplace at the far end, and the chimney was covered to force the smoke into the upstairs chamber. During hot weather, Harold's grandmother did much of her cooking over that fireplace to keep the house cool.

Five horses, hitched up to pull two sets of harrows, are preparing for spring planting on the Slingerland farm at Stony Hill, c. 1920. Amasa Slingerland is on the left. The little boy is his son, Harold. The hired man on the right is Roland Wagoner, a brother to Orcelia Willsey, who lived on what was then part of Delaware Turnpike, but is now Rock City Road near Clarksville.

The N.B. Houck Clarksville House, c. 1920, was owned by Isaac VanWie in the late 1850s. Isaac died in 1866, and his wife Mary VanWie became the new owner. Their son, Charles H. VanWie, ran a hardware store in the building. Later, Arthur Houck operated a hotel, followed by Nicholas B. Houck. Even later, James Brate operated a grocery store here with apartments upstairs. The building burned in the mid-1960s.

Myron B. Earl operated a general store in various locations in Clarksville for about 50 years. This building still stands near the intersection of Route 443 and Mill Street. This c. 1910 photograph shows Myron Earl in front of one of his first stores. Notice the *Killips Laundry* sign on the porch, the hitching post, and buggy at the side of the building. Myron Earl was also a teacher in Clarksville.

Clarksville's Central Hotel, seen here c. 1890, had a large ballroom, rooms for guests, and a dining room. James Houck owned the hotel that was later owned by John Fuller. Notice the slate sidewalks used at the time. On January 13, 1912, the Central Hotel burned down along with the confectionery store.

D.C. Gould is standing in front of his ice cream, soda, and confectionery store in Clarksville c. 1890. Gould also repaired clocks and watches. He was married to Mary Blodgett, the adopted daughter of Mr. and Mrs. Adam Clark (for whom Clarksville was named). The large barn to the right was the carriage shed and ballroom for the Central Hotel. The store burned in 1912 along with the Central Hotel.

Woodward's Helderberg Honey was produced by D.L. Woodward in Clarksville. The Woodwards lived in the Clark House, with the hives to the west of the house. The building on the right of the photograph was the honey house where they packaged the honey for sale. What appears to look like a culvert, to the left of the house, is the bee cellar. A home now stands over the bee cellar. The bees were initially moved to a Clipp Road location from the Woodward's original homestead in

Grooms Corners. They were later moved to Clarksville in 1917, when the Woodwards purchased the Clark House. The bee business continued until the early 1950s. While it operated, they had a showroom in the house and sold by mail order. Mr. Woodward was also a state bee inspector.

WOODWARD'S
HELDERBERG
HONEY
NET WEIGHT
8 OZ
PRODUCED BY
D. L. WOODWARD
CLARKSVILLE
N. Y.

Looking at this flock of sheep grazing on the knoll could make anyone envy their lifestyle, free of concerns. Their needs seem to be fulfilled by the warm sun, plentiful grass, and companionship for each other. Although scenes like this can still be seen, more farms in earlier times would have had their own sheep for meat and wool. This flock belonged to Anson Rowe near Clarksville, c. 1940. Bennett Hill can be seen to the left.

Clarksville farmers pitch hay onto a wagon at the Bennett Hill Farm in July 1924. The farmhouse was operated as a boardinghouse that was called the Bennett Hill House during this period. On the left is Frank Weidman from Slingerland Avenue. On the wagon is Peter Frederick, also from Slingerland Avenue. John Swart is standing next to the wagon wheel.

The Applebee Funeral Home, c. 1910, was located in the Clark House in Clarksville. Here, a horse-drawn hearse driven by Peter Frederick is parked along the side of the funeral home. Peter Applebee is standing to the right. The Clark House, a pillared Greek Revival-style home, was built by Adam Clark between 1826 and 1828. After the funeral home moved to a new location at the Clark Hotel, this home was purchased by D. Lester Woodward, a beekeeper, in 1917.

During WWII, many families pitched in and grew Victory Gardens. This large garden was tended by the Osterhout family near their Indian Ladder Lodge above New Salem, c. 1942. The people, from left to right, are as follows: Marilyn; Thomas; Grandpa Tom; Little Tom; Cookie (Wyman Jr.); Alice (in the wheelbarrow); Helen, Eunice, and Helena Osterhout; and Dorothy Wilsey. The present-day Route 85 is to the rear.

This early 1900s treadmill, operated by horse power, drives a saw blade in a wood-cutting operation in New Salem. Many cords of firewood were needed to heat a home for the long winter. The exact location has not been determined.

This set of barns, belonging to Hiram Martin, was located on the north side of New Scotland Road near New Salem, c. 1925. Hiram's son, Harvey, is pictured here with his horses. The barn is typical of the Dutch-style buildings that were built in the New Scotland area. The open side of the lower barn was an easy place for the horses to take cover. Notice the chicken having its freedom to roam at will. The barn burned in the early 1950s.

This 1912 barn raising at the William Truax farm, north of Hiram Martin's farm, shows the use of post-and-beam construction. Farmers from all around the area came to help with this project. This barn was 80 feet long and 45 feet wide with a slate roof. The builder was Frank Osterhout, a noted area barn builder. The barn continued in use on the Badgley farm from 1936 to 1955. It was removed in 1973.

Some of the workers at the Truax barn raising in 1912 enjoy a lunch break. Barn raisings, a neighborhood project, was common throughout New Scotland a century ago. The women would prepare the huge noonday meal to serve all the men working on the barn. Sometimes doors from the house were put on sawhorses to provide temporary tables. Notice the sheet used to provide some shade for the men.

This "buck rake" was built by the driver, Jerry Badgley, in the early 1940s to bring in the hay. Farm machinery was hard to get during wartime, and Cornell advisors came out and advised many farmers on buck rake assembly. The back had wooden "rakes" that lowered with a power take-off. The machine was backed into the windrows of hay until it was full. The rakes would then be lifted again and the load driven to the barn. This photograph dates to 1943.

Neal's Diner, as it appeared in the late 1950s, was located across from the Indian Ladder Drive-in on Route 85. This diner replaced an earlier roadside stand, also run by Chester Neal. The diner was known for its seafood on Friday nights. It closed in the early 1980s and has since been torn down.

The Youmans Farm, located on Youmans Road in New Scotland, shows a barn and milk house in 1935. The farm trucks were a 1934 Ford and a 1935 Chevrolet. These were used to deliver milk in Albany. The barn was built by A.C. Youmans, a minister, around 1907. A.C.'s son, Lester, began working the farm full time in 1914, establishing their very successful retail milk business in Albany.

James Wayne was the owner of the Capitol View Farm, located one-quarter of a mile west of Swift Road in New Scotland, c. 1900. Mr. Wayne was a prominent dairy farmer in the New Scotland area. He is holding the bull with a bull staff, which is fastened to the ring in the bull's nose. This device allowed him to handle the bull with relative safety. The home on this farm remains today, but the barns were removed by Lester Youmans in 1936.

63

This photograph was taken inside the office of Ackerman's New Scotland coal business, which was across from Crear's Store. It was located east of the underpass on what is now Route 85. Seated at the desk is Ed Carhart with Jay Whitbeck seated on the left. Note the prices of coal listed above the desk. Judging by the telephone and other furnishings, we date the photograph to around 1940. This business was first established by Jay's father, Andrew J. Whitbeck, in the late 19th century. Jay Whitbeck lost his hand in a hunting accident.

Hay, flour, feed, and groceries were sold here by Jay Whitbeck until the early 1920s. In 1926, it then became Crear's Store, which also housed the post office. When the new road was built in 1949, the store was cut off because the street became a dead end. At the time of construction, a temporary road was built to the rear of the store and over the grade crossing. The building has been vacant for many years. This postcard is dated 1911.

This garage was originally a blacksmith shop in New Scotland. By 1920, it had become a garage and gas station. In 1930, Lauren Kisselburg took over the garage. He built a larger garage down the road in 1936, the year this photograph was taken. To the left of the garage is the New Scotland Schoolhouse, currently the New Scotland town hall.

Lauren Kisselburg certainly expanded his business with his new Kissel's Garage in 1936. He had a successful towing business and repair garage. Pictured in 1950, from left to right, are Lauren Kisselburg, ? Ingleston, Mrs. Sholder, Joe Loucks, Diane Kisselburg, Bob Moak, and Bud Neiman. After Lauren's death in 1973, his wife continued to run the garage until 1998.

JOSEPH HILTON & SONS,

BREEDERS OF

Registered Devon Cattle,

NEW SCOTLAND,

ALBANY CO., N. Y.

FARM 1½ MILES FROM VOORHEESVILLE—JUNCTION OF THE WEST SHORE AND D. & H. C. CO.'S R. R.

The large red barn on the Colony Country Club's Maple Road property near Voorheesville is all that remains of the once large and prosperous Hilton Farm. The barn was built by Frank Osterhout in 1897. The house was to the left of the barn. The first Hiltons raised sheep in the 1790s. Much later, Joseph Hilton became a well-known breeder of Registered Devon Cattle. This advertising card dates to *c.* 1900.

This garage in Voorheesville, pictured in 1966, was originally owned by Joe Watson, who ran it until the early 1950s. To the right, the outdoor automotive lift can be seen, a common sight in the 1930s and 1940s. The concrete building was the service station for the garage. This building was rented to the Voorheesville School from 1942 to 1950 for school shop classes (see page 103). The Mobil Corporation replaced both buildings in the fall of 1966.

J.E. Carpenter's store, located on South Main Street in Voorheesville, was built in the late 1800s. It later became Schaefer's Store and in the 1920s it became Ricci's Market, which operated until December 1987. In 1925, the barn on the left was torn down. The Ricci family used the lumber from the barn to build a porch on the front of the building.

This Tydol station in Voorheesville, c. 1930, was owned by Leonard Smith and, later, by his brother Frank. During WWII, Frank's wife, Lil, sat in the station or their home upstairs and wrote letters to all the servicemen from the Voorheesville area. The garage was later owned by Mac McGann. "Honest Mike" Frohlich purchased the garage in 1951 and operated it until his death in 1974. His son, Richard, continued to operate it until 1980. A Stewart's shop is on the site now.

The Albany Malleable Iron Works Foundry was located on Foundry Road in Voorheesville. This was built in 1908. Note that the water tower on the right was still incomplete at the time this photograph was taken, c. 1915. This business later became Albany Castings Company, which closed in the early 1960s. Over the years, it employed as many as 200 people.

The Empire Cider and Vinegar Works in Voorheesville, c. 1900, began operations in 1890. In 1917, this was purchased and operated by Duffy Mott until it closed in 1956. Many local farmers sold their surplus apples here. The business also provided many jobs for the local residents. As is apparent here, the railroad was convenient for shipping Duffy Mott products to market.

This was the aftermath of the 1954 fire at O.B. Vunck's Feedmill in Voorheesville. The entire building was destroyed. A new mill, which had concrete firewalls and state-of-the-art equipment, was built on the site. In October 1957, that mill was destroyed in a spectacular blaze that could be seen from Albany. Five trains were held up by the blaze, and 600 tons of feed were lost. George Vunck, the owner of the mill and mayor of Voorheesville, did not rebuild.

LaGrange Falls, pictured in 1907, is located near the junction of the present-day Krumkill and Normanskill Roads on the Vly Creek. The original LaGrange family purchased the land in 1711 and built a sawmill here around 1720. A gristmill, which had three large grinding stones and was connected to the sawmill, was later erected in 1831. Many tons of buckwheat flour were ground here yearly. The mill can be seen on the right above the falls.

In 1960, Niagara Mohawk purchased a 450-foot right of way, bisecting the town from north to south. The landscape changed dramatically when they cleared this land and built the new power lines. Farms were cut in half. In June 1961, two homes on Towne Lane near Voorheesville had to be moved to new locations, as this photograph illustrates. In 1972, the right of way was widened on the east side and the huge metal towers were added.

Four

TRANSPORTATION

This car is attempting to negotiate Koonz Road near the Weidman home. Beginning on February 15 and continuing for three days, the third storm to hit the area in rapid succession became known as the "Blizzard of '58." There were gigantic drifts when the winds finally stopped, and roads were closed for days. Operation Snowbound began on February 18 at the county highway department near Voorheesville. Helicopters loaded with food, fuel, hay, and medical supplies departed for the snowbound hilltowns for five days. The Red Cross and volunteers from the area pitched in to pack supplies. This chapter will show the various means of transportation used in different time periods.

This Feura Bush railroad station, as it looked in the late 1800s, was built c. 1870. Later on, a matching extension was added on the left side of the building. In addition to handling agricultural products, mail, and regular passengers, the train carried students to Ravena for high school classes for many years. The station ceased to operate around 1940. Will Vadney was a stationmaster there in the 1920s.

This blacksmith shop, located on Route 301 east of the Onesquethaw Reformed church, was operated by George Latta, c. 1900. Many generations of the Latta family operated this shop since the early 19th century. With changing times, it became a gas station until it was destroyed by fire in the 1960s. Neighbors remember Mobil gas being hand-pumped here. The last owner and operator was Fred Latta.

People would use a horse and sleigh to provide transportation and pleasure in the winter. On February 1, 1942, Earl LaGrange and his son, Ronald, arrived at the Slingerland farm by pony and cutter for a neighborly Sunday afternoon visit. The building in the background was the wagon house on the Slingerland farm. It was destroyed by fire in 1947.

March, with its warm days and cold nights, was a busy month for many folks when the sap began to run in the maple trees. They gathered the sap in the woods and often used a team of horses and a sled to bring it to the sugarhouse. Here, it was boiled and eventually became maple syrup. Maple syrup and other maple products often supplemented the income of local farmers. This photograph was taken c. 1940.

The William H. Bradt family, all dressed up, are probably on their way to services at the Unionville Church, c. 1880. The children are John Vanderhyden Bradt, born on January 5, 1873, and his sister, Anna E., born on August 19, 1875. There was a younger child, Emma, who was born on July 1, 1877. Mrs. Bradt was the former Ella Jones. The home in the rear is located on Brownrigg Road.

This motorized bus was known as "the stage." Notice the solid rubber tires. There were many boardinghouses in the Clarksville area, and many tourists from Albany arrived on this bus. The bus traveled from Albany to Clarksville and then on to Thompsons Lake. The building in the background is Myron B. Earl's store in Clarksville. This postcard dates to 1909.

A steam engine and its crew are shown in a rock quarry on the Amasa Slingerland farm. During the 1920s, when the Delaware Turnpike was being rebuilt, the stone quarried here was used as a foundation for the road. Nearby was a foundation for the scales where the horse-drawn wagons were weighed, first empty, and then loaded with stone.

Bert VanWie is climbing into his "car," which appears to be part pick-up truck, on Slingerlands Avenue, Clarksville in 1913. Notice that the steering wheel is on the right. Seated in the front seat is Martha Flansburg with her sister, Fannie, behind her, both visitors to the area. The woman in the center is Bert's wife, Carrie. In the background is Peter Frederick's house.

Someone appears to be walking across the old Iron Bridge (called the McIntosh Bridge) over the Onesquethaw Creek as it looked in the early 1900s. Clarksville is to the left. The buildings to the left belong to the McIntosh family. The barn in the rear on the right no longer exists.

This winter scene was photographed by Anson Rowe in 1932 from the north side of the new bridge. The original drawing for the bridge states, "The Oniskethau Creek Bridge at Clarksville, NY; 1931 April 30th, Designed by Babcock Bros., 55 W 42nd St. N. Y. City; Approved Wm. R. Gordon, County Superintendent of Highways." The bridge was built in 1932 under the Work Projects Administration (WPA) program. Edgar S. McIntosh and his son, Willis McIntosh Sr., built the forms. John Lounsbury was the stone mason.

A walking suspension bridge was located over the upper gorge of the Onesquethaw Creek near Clarksville, *c.* 1900. The bridge was built *c.* 1890 by George C. Ingraham as a shortcut from the family farm on Bennett Hill to the village. He was assisted by his cousins who lived in the Houck neighborhood. Later, George worked as a surveyor.

The Town of New Scotland Highway Department purchased its first steam roller *c.* 1925. From left to right are William Elmendorf, George Glasser, Elton Blessing, Culbert Woodworth, Frank Hallenbeck, John Blessing, and George Zeh. In the cab are Mel Russo and Harry Allen.

This postcard shows the "Letter S," *c.* 1900, as it climbs the Helderberg range near Clarksville. In the 19th century, this area was cleared for farming. Because of this, the road's S-shape could easily be observed. It turned out that the land was unsuitable for farming and much of it has returned to forest. Many of the sharper curves have been removed as well, so we no longer get this panoramic view.

The West Shore Railroad Station, *c.* 1900, was located on the west side of the tracks in New Scotland. The track was built in 1865 from Athens to Schenectady. It later became the New York Central Railroad. There was passenger and freight service. Frazee and Company shipped hay and straw, and the Bender Farm shipped melons. Coal arrived here for Whitbeck's Coal Pocket. Mail was also dropped and picked up here. The station closed *c.* 1925 and no longer remains.

The New Scotland Road project, begun in 1949, diverted Route 85 to the right from the old road. This September 1950 photograph shows a view looking east. In the foreground is where the railroad underpass is now, replacing an earlier underpass at the same location. Long Lumber is to the right. The house, belonging to Don Sutton (later Long's), was moved out of the way of the roadway. On the left, the Mobil sign at Crear's Store can be seen.

A Delaware and Hudson passenger train is stopped in its tracks on its way to Voorheesville from Albany after a snowstorm in 1917. This photograph was taken at Hilton's Crossing on Hilton Road and shows that even a powerful steam engine could be slowed by Mother Nature.

This vehicle was known as a "doodlebug." Vehicles like this were popular around town and in the country during the 1930s and 1940s, when times were hard. A doodlebug was made by finding spare parts from old trucks and cars and making a new device that would get them around. Sometimes, chains were fitted for winter use. The driver is John Hallenbeck, and George Bidwell is on the left. Both were from Voorheesville.

Frank VanAuken of Voorheesville often referred to this vehicle, c. 1910, as a "thing-a-ma-jig." It is a 1900 Knox that would remain in his family for almost one hundred years. It ran on a one-cylinder, air-cooled engine, and had three wheels. The front wheel was tubeless and the rear wheels were solid tires. It had two speeds, no reverse, a tiller for steering, and would go eight miles per hour.

Bill Munyan is pumping gas, *c.* 1950, at his garage on Maple Avenue, Voorheesville. In 1933, he purchased the garage from his sister-in-law, Frances McLaury (Patton), and ran it until the early 1960s. The garage was originally owned by his father-in-law, Guy McLaury, until he died in 1927. Frances ran the garage for five years. Her mechanic was Wesley Jacobson Sr., who had worked for her father. Mr. Munyan began driving the first school bus in Voorheesville in 1939.

A winter wonderland can be seen at the intersection of Voorheesville Avenue and Main Street in front of the Frank Smith's Tydol station on January 28, 1945. The sign on the bus to the left reads, "Albany Castings Company" and was used to bring workers from Albany to that busy factory during the war. The other bus is a United Traction Company bus that took over from Frank Hungerford's company in Voorheesville in 1942.

Union Station in Voorheesville can be seen c. 1898, before it was enlarged. The cider mill is in the distance on the left. There is a boardwalk that goes around the station and down to the tracks to the right. This station was built in 1889 by two railroads: the Albany & Susquehanna and the Saratoga & Hudson River Railroads. It replaced a structure dating to 1865.

After being enlarged around 1900, the Voorheesville Railroad Station had a new look. This photograph was taken by Ed Relyea from the top of a boxcar in the late 1950s. Note the platform of the freight house in the foreground. The Grove Hotel is beyond the station.

This D & H steam locomotive is crossing the tracks in Voorheesville, c. 1900. You can see the pointed roof of the station, the freight building and the park. To the rear of the park, you can see the end of the block of South Main Street before the last section, the flatiron part, was built. This has often been mistaken for the Harris House. The photograph was taken from the end of Foundry Road.

A team of horses brings supplies to the workers while the steam shovel digs the ditch for the new Voorheesville water line. This picture was taken on Route 85A in 1923 near the present Frohlich home. The water line was coming from the Livingston Springs on Martin Road.

This picture reminds us of the good practice of "neighbor helping neighbor." The wooden sleigh belonged to Charlie Livingston. He was coming down Route 85A and picking up friends to attend services at the Methodist Church in Voorheesville during the winter of 1926. Fur coats and blankets were certainly a priority for these rides. It may have been cold, but it was better than walking.

This bridge, which is next to the Myndert Crounse farm (now Winchell's farm) on New Salem Road, collapsed in September 1938 when its supports were washed out. Fortunately, no one was on the bridge at the time. Evident in the picture are the planks that were put in place to walk across. There was much flooding throughout the town as a result of torrential rains from a hurricane.

Five

SCHOOLS, CHURCHES, AND ORGANIZATIONS

Schools, churches, and various organizations were at the center of social life in each hamlet of the town throughout the late 19th and first half of the 20th century. This school in Onesquethaw, c. 1920, was located across the road from the Onesquethaw Reformed church and was in use until the 1940s. Built in 1869, it had three rooms, two of which were small and located on both sides of the front door. One room held coats, boots, and lunches; the other was a playroom. A woodstove heated the building with the families supplying the wood. Behind the school were two outhouses, one for boys and one for girls. Some of the families who went here included the VanDykes, McNabs, Vanderbilts, Crounses, VanHoesens, Osterhouts, Argeris, Wisenburns, Kawczaks, Groesbecks, and Rowes.

This Feura Bush School, District No. 5, was dedicated on January 3, 1885 for grades one through eight. The school remained in use until 1929 and has seen many other uses, including an automobile garage for the parsonage. It is currently the Feura Bush Library, which was organized by the Feura Bush Neighborhood Association in 1987. Despite all these changes, the old blackboards still remain in place.

These boys and girls pose in front of the Feura Bush School in April 1918. Note the original doors. The children, from left to right, are as follows: (front row) Ken Bain, Martin Wickham, Sarah Martin, Carolyn Hallenbeck, Anna Wright, Grace Martin, Harmon Tryon; (middle row) George Alberts, J. Bain, Dorothy Holman, Charles Johnson, Mike Waldenmaier, William Hakes, Clint Wagner, Ruth Milleit, Marjorie Moak; (back row) Frances Northrup, Gladys Vadney, Lillian Wright, Pearl Wright, Frank Vadney, Milo Vanderveer, Gladys Hakes, Miss Leona Patrie, Florence Heller, Claude Tryon.

The Jerusalem Reformed church in Feura Bush was built in 1825. It had box-style pews with doors and a gallery extending around three sides. In 1844, a horse shed containing 12 stalls was added to the property. In 1871, the building was lengthened by 17 feet as pictured. Note the carriage block near the entrance that was used by parishioners arriving to church. At the time the church was built, Feura Bush was known as Jerusalem.

A Feura Bush School picnic, c. 1925, was held along the Onesquethaw Creek. The area was owned by A. VanDerzee at the time. Standing in the rear is the teacher, Louise Billington. The children posing are, from left to right, as follows: (kneeling) unidentified, unidentified, Estell Parrot, unidentified, unidentified, Anna Wright, unidentified; (standing) Amber Alberts, unidentified, unidentified, Elwood Vadney, John Heller, Raymond Northrup, Kenneth Wright, unidentified, unidentified, and unidentified.

This brick school in Feura Bush was opened in 1929 for grades one through eight. The school had four classrooms but only two were used most of the time. Louise Billington taught grades one through four, and Edith Cornell had grades five through eight. The school served the community with an active PTA. Dances, plays, and card parties took place. Basketball games were played in the gym even though the ceiling did not meet regulation height. The school closed c. 1950.

Feura Bush became part of the Onesquethaw Fire District in 1939. This truck is a 1942 Dodge. The firemen in this c. 1944 photograph are, from left to right, as follows: (top) Pat Heinz, unidentified; (standing) Howard Vadney, George Billington, Dewey Vadney, Sam Millet, Henry Wyrick, Dave Rothaupt, Ray Vadney, Donald Bushey, Dewey Rothaupt; (front) Victor Miller, and John Heller. Dewey Rothaupt's garage was the first Ford dealership in Albany County. The garage, built in 1935, was removed in 1985 to make way for the post office.

Elsie Vanderbilt Stott and her daughter, Clara May Stott (Marsh), enjoy a carriage ride to church, c. 1916. The carriage would have been kept in the carriage shed during the service. This is the Onesquethaw Reformed Church in Tarrytown. It was built in 1825 with the stones that were rejected from the construction of the Erie Canal because they were too small. The clock on the steeple is only a painted face. There is no clock mechanism.

This picture of the old Unionville School, District No. 13, was taken c. 1898. It is obvious that the building was past its prime. It stood on the steep part (note the foundation) of the Unionville Hill, just below the present-day fire hall. The large wooden bin in front of the building was for coal and wood. The teacher was Elias White from the Berne area.

The new Unionville School, *c.* 1910, was built east of the church in 1907. The old schoolhouse was sold at auction to Lewis Edinger for $32.50. Van LaGrange's diary for September 7, 1907, states, "moving seats from old school to new." Miss Barton was the first teacher here. After the district became part of Bethlehem Central, this building became a private home.

Pictured here is the interior of the new Unionville School as it looked in 1920. Note the stovepipe in the upper left, the ink bottles, and the school clock. The teacher was Natalie Hopper Attwood. She was born in New Jersey but spent most of her life in this area. She first taught in the Stony Hill School but spent many more years at Unionville. The Attwoods lived on the first farm that you would come to heading south on the Unionville-Feura Bush Road.

A proud 4H member, Harold Slingerland, c. 1930, prepares his Guernsey heifer for showing at the Altamont Fair. If the heifer did well at that fair, she would probably go on to the state fair. Conditioning involved keeping the animal brushed and spotlessly clean, with a bleached tail, and polished hooves and horns. She would be blanketed to keep her coat soft. She and her owner would learn good show ring behavior. Many boys and girls throughout the town were 4H members.

This aerial view of the Unionville Reformed church, built in 1825, was taken soon after the one-story extension was built on the back in 1957. This addition provided more room for Sunday school classes and social events, as well as for indoor plumbing. The horse sheds were erected in 1840. They are the only ones still surviving in Albany County.

The Methodist Society of Clarksville was organized in 1856. This building was constructed in 1858 on the land that was purchased on the south side of Delaware Turnpike, west of Plank Road. A parsonage, which still stands, was built on the left and to the rear of the same lot in 1883. This church served the community until the 1960s, when the Clarksville Community Church was built and this structure was demolished. This photograph dates to *c.* 1953.

This photograph of garden produce was taken at the Altamont Fair Grange exhibit, *c.* 1925. The basket of roses at the top center of the picture were grown by Clara Weidman from Slingerland Avenue in Clarksville. The sign reads "Clarksville Grange 781 P of H" (Patrons of Husbandry).

AN
ARIZONA COWBOY

———

A Comedy-Drama of the Great Southwest
in Four Acts

Presented By

The Clarksville Grange
Friday Evening, Dec. 15, 1933, at 8:00 P. M.

———

CAST of CHARACTERS

Leroy Vanderbilt......Farley Gantt	....	The Cowboy Sheriff
Harold Slingerlands ...Paul Quillian	....	His Partner
Edgar Kukuk......Duke Blackshear	....	A Stranger from Frisco
Floyd Gates......Hezekiah Bugg	....	A Glorious Liar
John Mudge.........Yow Kee	...........A Heathen Chinee	
Frank Kukuk.........Big Elk	.............A Navajo Chief	
Leo Appleby...........Grizzly Grimm	.............A Cattle Thief	
Clara Stott.........Marguerite Moore	..... The Pretty Ranch Owner	
Elsie Stott..........Mrs. Petunia Bugg...........From Old Indianny		
Dorothy Gould........Coralie Blackshear.................Duke's Sister		
Elena Appleby......Fawn Afraid	..........An Indian Maid	
Ruth Hopkins......Young'un	.... Not Much of Anybody	

Cowboys

SCENES

Act I. Exterior of the Palace Hotel, Purple Dog, Arizona. A morning in October.

Act II. Same scene, afternoon of the same day.

Act III. Same as Acts I and II.

Act IV. A Cave in the mountains.

Time of Playing - About Two and One-Quarter Hours.

A playbill, dated 1933, identifies one of the many plays put on at Grange Hall over the years. The Clarksville Grange No. 781 was chartered in 1893. Alexander Flansburg joined the Grange in 1893 and was soon elected master. He was instrumental in the purchase of the Grange Hall building in 1896. Previously, the building had housed several different stores. The Grange closed in September 1969.

The Clarksville Reformed church, c. 1910, was built early in 1854 on the corner of Delaware Turnpike and North Road. On a cold and windy day—February 4, 1912, right after services had been held—the alarm went through the town that this structure was burning. Bucket brigades were kept busy saving buildings on a nearby farm; the church was a total loss.

This is the church that was immediately erected on the same lot after the original Clarksville Reformed church had burned in February 1912. The new building was dedicated on May 30, 1913, and stood until the 1960s when the Clarksville Community church was built and this structure was torn down.

These young ladies of the New Salem Reformed Church are dressed up for a patriotic playlet in 1917. The leader is Mrs. William Higgins. The girls, from left to right, are Dorothy Erwin (Rock), Irene Albright, Katherine Hallenbeck, Adelaide Albright, Audrey Crabill (Boyle), Mildred Albright, Nellie Bloomingdale (Sheehan), Annabelle Young, and Eliza Allen (Stoneburner).

This c. 1925 photograph shows the Ouray Tribe No. 480 of the Improved Order of Red Men of New Salem in their ceremonial sashes. Congress chartered this non-profit organization after the Revolutionary War. Many community activities took place at Red Men Hall over the years. This building was originally the Methodist church.

Thirty-seven children and their teacher pose outside the New Salem one-room school in 1883. School records show that in addition to four electric lights, water from Bethlehem was installed in 1929. Because of increased enrollment, residents of the New Salem district voted to add another room at the cost of $7,000. This room was completed in 1941. The New Salem School closed in 1960 and the children were then enrolled in the Voorheesville School.

The New Salem School, District No. 4, which housed grades one through eight, is shown as it appeared in 1918. The coatroom was in the rear with a door to the outside. The stove-pipe in the rear appears to be new. The windows on the left remain in the museum today, as well as the original floor and blackboards. Harvey Martin, Elizabeth Hallenbeck, and Ella Hallenbeck are known to have been in this class.

96

Forty-six children pose in the grass behind the New Salem one-room schoolhouse in 1937. They are, from left to right, as follows: (front row) John Caswell, Gordon Tarrington, Carol Simpkins, Alfred Higgins, Earl MacMillen; (second row) Lois Sharp, Amy Stoneburner, Alfreda Charlebois, Marion MacMillen, Eleanor Klapp, Vivian Alger, Ilene Martin, Beulah MacMillen, Frances Klapp, Jean Reissman, Lillian Sharp, Catherine Caswell; (third row) ? Duell, Marietta Klapp, Bernice Reissman, Anna Berschwinger, Nina Countryman, Esther Houk, Judy Bean, Pauline Charlebois, Edith Reissman, Leslie Willis, Charlotte Fischer, Ella Duell; (fourth row) Arthur Wetmiller, Kenneth Sisson, Rene Charlebois, Dean Willis, Walter Osterhout, ? Duell, Orville Countryman, Leonard Berschwinger, Wyman "Cookie" Osterhout, Wayland Rivenburg, Fred Berschwinger, Kenneth Warner; (fifth row) unidentified, Raymond Conger, unidentified, Alden Countryman, and Walter Miller. Mrs. Chesebro taught grades one through four. Mrs. Sisson taught grades five through eight. The two teachers shared one room.

This New Salem Reformed church, c. 1910, was built in 1893. It replaced a church built on this site in 1875. The church was first organized in 1783. Parishioners met in homes and barns for many years. The first church building was built west of its present location in 1813, and that was replaced in 1845. The locally well-known Reverend Harmanus VanHuysen was pastor here from 1793 to 1824. The church, a longtime center of community life, closed in December 1998.

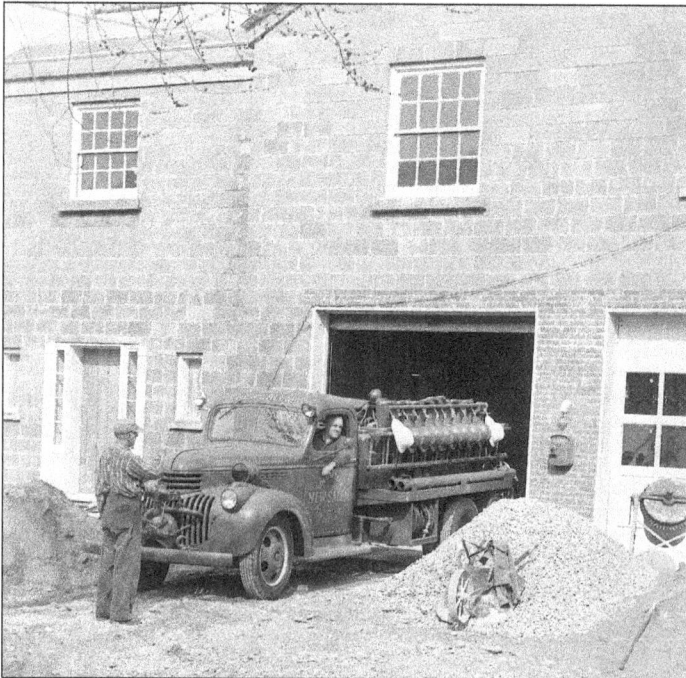

Shortly after WWII, the returning veterans and the New Salem Patriotic Association created the volunteer fire department. This photograph shows the New Salem firehouse when it was almost completed in 1949. Captain Peter Winne is backing the truck into the firehouse under the watchful eye of fireman Arthur Winne. The truck is a 1942 Chevrolet purchased from government surplus for $900. Before being housed in this building, the truck was stored in the New Salem garage.

In this picture, a Boy Scout troop is on its way to a camp-out carrying their bedrolls, *c.* 1915. They were standing at the intersection of Plank Road and North Road in New Salem. The carriage shed of the New Salem Hotel, with the dance hall overhead, can be seen. The last three scouts on the right are Aden Crabill, Ross Erwin, and Harold Higgins.

This is the Clipp Road School in District No. 7 as it appeared in 1914, when Elizabeth Wynkoop was the teacher. Mrs. Edna Bashford taught for about 20 years in this school before it closed. She continued teaching in Voorheesville until she retired in 1959. The Clipp Road School closed and was sold in 1941 to the man who owned the land where the school was located. The Turnpike Rod and Gun Club used the building from 1956 until 1967. Notice the rope swing.

The New Scotland Presbyterian Church was organized in 1787. It is the oldest church in the town, with the first building having been erected in 1791. The present-day church was built in 1849 with additions and renovations since. The tiffany stained glass window was moved here from the Voorheesville Presbyterian church. The church is located in the hamlet of New Scotland on New Scotland Road. There is an old cemetery beside the church.

The New Scotland School, District No. 8, seen here c. 1920, was built in 1866. Prior to this, a log school had occupied this site since 1804. The building ceased being a school in 1952. It was renovated for use as the New Scotland town hall in May 1957. Several additions have been added since that time.

This picture was taken inside the New Scotland School in 1943. Those shown, from left to right, are as follows: (front row) Arthur Bement, unidentified, unidentified, Clifton Smith, Phillip Irwin, Clint Wagner, Bob Wagner; (second row) Billie Zautner, Carol Hallenbeck, Barbara Connell, unidentified, unidentified, unidentified, Judy Salisbury, unidentified, Nancy Booth, Keith Ackerman; (back row) Harland Davis, Herbie Moak, Diane Kisselberg, Joan Wagner, Charlotte Connell, Sally Zautner, Donny Zautner, and unidentified. The teacher, Jane Blessing, taught here from 1932 until the school closed in 1952

Pictured in her uniform is Helen F. Parker of Voorheesville. She was a local Red Cross worker during WWI, c. 1918. She was the mother of Allison Bennett, a prominent local historian. New Scotland women were very active in the Red Cross. The minutes from Red Cross meetings at the New Scotland Church from June 1918 to April 1919 reveal that the women made property bags, operating gowns, socks, camisoles, quilts, and hospital shirts. Also mentioned was their involvement in Belgian relief work.

This 1926 Child's fire truck was purchased March 1928 for $5,000 and is operated by Homer Corbin, the Voorheesville fire chief from 1932 to 1941. The truck was sold in August 1951 for $400 to the Lake Desolation Fire Department. In 1969, it was purchased back for $233 and the firemen have since restored it for use at parades and conventions. The Voorheesville Hose Company No. One was organized in 1901.

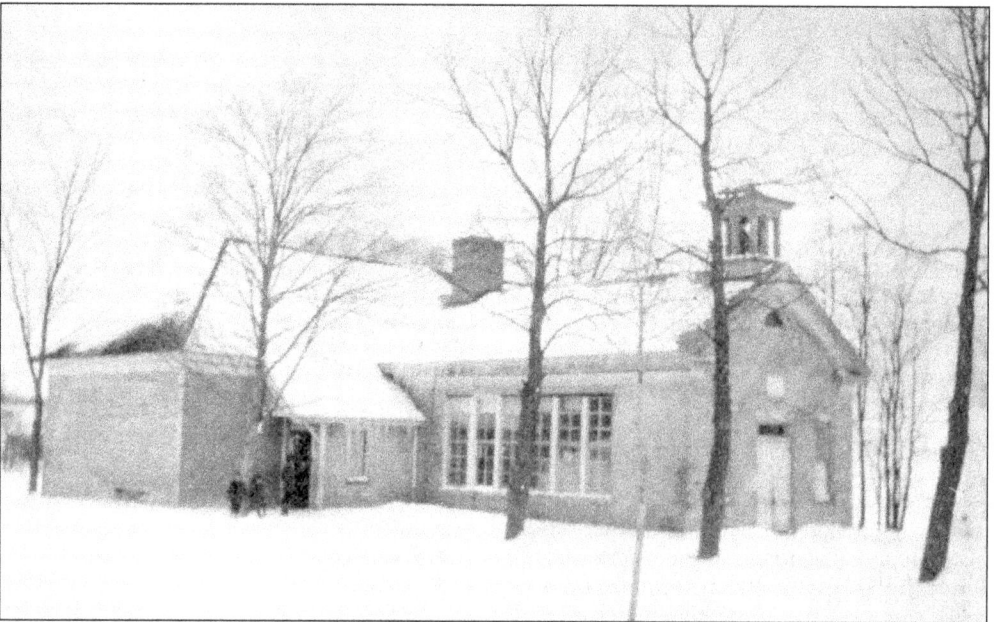

The first log school built in Voorheesville (1826) was replaced by the front portion of this brick building in 1867. An additional room was added in 1892, followed by a third room in 1911. The building pictured was used until 1930 when the present-day brick building was built behind it. With completion of that building, this one was torn down. This school was often called "Brookview Academy" because it was next to the Vly Creek.

This was Voorheesville's eighth grade graduating class of 1930. Those shown, from left to right, are as follows: (seated) Bernard Pafunda, Evelyn Vosburg, Mr. Clayton Bouton, Bernadette Alkenbrack, Teddy Dluski; (standing) V. Tymchyn, Ernie Resue, Steve Bunk, Stewart McLaury, B. Garrison, Grover Kling. In 1921, Mr. Bouton came to Voorheesville after three years in the Clarksville School. As principal, he helped the school develop from a three-room school to a large district by the time he retired in 1963. In 1958, the new junior-senior high school was named for him.

Dave McCartney (the shop teacher) and Eleanor Busier (the school nurse serving all the schools in the district) are seen inside the old Voorheesville school shop on Maple Avenue next to Smith's Tavern (see page 67). Dave, called "Mac," was the first shop teacher in the district, serving from 1942 until his retirement in 1977. Miss Busier retired in 1967. The old shop had a coal-burning furnace. One of Mac's jobs was to keep the fire burning.

The Voorheesville Volunteer Fire Department is shown in this 1937 photograph. The firemen, from left to right, are as follows: (front row) Mike Pafunda, John Kammerer, Charlie Ricci, Frank Person, Frank Osterhout, Charlie Fields; (middle row) Elmer Boynton, Frank Smith, Don Sutherland, O. Ward, Otto Schultz, Harold Pitcher, Jess Lasher, Clyde Loss, R. Flansburg, L. Chesebro, Ken D'Arpino, Mike Ulion, Gene Brown, Wes Jacobson Jr., Benny Thomas, Burt Halstead, Bill Munyan, Herb Young; (back row) Raymond Raynsford, Pete Zeh, E. Albright, Bill Schultz, Wes Jacobson, Hayley Ethridge, Charlie Curlette. The child is Alfred Pafunda.

Boy Scouts have always been very active in the Voorheesville area. This troop in the early 1930s includes, from left to right, the following: (front row) Ernest Resue, Bruce Herwig, Melvin Mead and Donald Spore, (back row) George Vunck, Harold Mead, Jack Herwig, Tom Crocker, and Stuart McLaury. George Vunck later became the mayor of Voorheesville. Harold Mead was a schoolteacher in Voorheesville for many years.

Virginia Smith Pitcher Maxwell, Evelyn VanWormer Freer, and Marguerite Joslin are performing the play *Six Who Passed While the Lentils Boiled* for their Girl Scout troop in Voorheesville, *c.* 1925. Their performance earned them the Dramatics Badge. Most of the emphasis was on earning badges. This troop also worked on the Laundress Badge, and some girls cleaned a house in Albany to earn the Housekeeper Badge.

The Voorheesville Presbyterian church, seen here c. 1920, was erected in 1886 on Main Street. The manse for the church is on the hill in the background. The church, having disbanded in 1940, housed a classroom for the Voorheesville School near the end of that decade. From 1950 to February 1989, it was the home of the Voorheesville Public Library. During the 1950s, the basement of the building was a canteen for the teenagers of the area. The building is currently a restaurant.

The First Methodist church in Voorheesville, c. 1900, originally stood on Altamont Road. Because of the location of the railroad, the center of the community changed. As a result, members of the church dismantled it in 1890 and moved it to its present site. The first service held at the new location was for Isaac VanAuken, who died of injuries he suffered while moving the church. The original social hall was over the carriage sheds behind the sanctuary.

106

St. Matthew's church, c. 1940, on Center Street in Voorheesville, was built in 1916 and dedicated in 1917. There were 30 active families at that time. Because it was a Mission Church, a priest had to travel from St. Lucy's in Altamont (occasionally from LaSalette) for services for almost 46 years. It was a Mission Church until April 27, 1962, when the new church on Mountain View Street was opened.

The Voorheesville ambulance passes Noticks department store during the Memorial Day parade in 1956. The Voorheesville Men's Club initiated the first ambulance drive in 1951. They raised $6,030.78 for the newly formed ambulance squad. The ambulance they purchased for $4,500 was a 1951 Cadillac. Initially, there were 17 charter members on the squad. This first ambulance was housed in John Heller's garage on Center Street. The present ambulance building was erected in 1960.

The Font Grove Schoolhouse, District No. 12, on Font Grove Road is shown here as it appeared in 1938. In the front row, on the left, is Suzanna Waldbilling. On the left in the back row are Agnes DeAngelis and Marie Genovesi. The school was in use until the early 1940s. It was later made into a home and burned in 1986.

The Tygert Road School, c. 1920, is also known as the Locust Vale School. Because of its location, it often experienced flooding. In a 1983 interview, Esther (Crounse) Schultz related the story of one such flood: the older boys had boots and carried the smaller children to the road. They then pulled the teacher, who was Esther's mother, Olive Truax Crounse, out on the sled. The building, now a home, has been relocated on the corner of Meadowdale and Altamont Road.

Six

RECREATION

This photograph presents a view looking east towards New Scotland from the Thacher Park overlook in 1952. In 1921, a party of government officials visited the park to test a new high-power searchlight. The light was set up on the cliff edge with the beam projecting onto the land below. The unobstructed view for many miles was favorable to the experiment and the test was successful. The small tower on the cliff's edge is no longer there. Besides Thacher Park, each hamlet offered a variety of recreational activities for the residents.

This photograph, taken in August 1912, shows Lawsons Lake. Only a small area of the lake falls within the borders of New Scotland. The lake was a big attraction in the early 1900s for fishing, boating, and walking. There was a large dock that offered boat rentals. Pictured, from left to right, are Dorothy Flansburg, Emeline Allen, Sarah Flansburg (mother of the girls), Frances Flansburg, and Martha Flansburg.

This is a small quarry on the Amasa Slingerland farm, from which stone was taken in the 1920s as a base for road improvements on Delaware Turnpike. At this time, the sharp curve was taken out of the road on the Unionville Hill. The holes that were drilled in the ledge for blasting powder can still be seen. The smooth rock floor that was left made a convenient place for family picnics. This couple camped here one summer.

A Unionville Church crew is shown washing barrels of clams in the water of the Onesquethaw Creek along Lower Flat Rock Road, c. 1937. The two boys are Everett and Donald Jones. Amasa Slingerland is on the left, John Mathias on the right. Elmer Jones's truck was backed into the streambed. People sometimes drove their cars here to wash them.

2nd
TWENTY-FIRST ANNUAL CLAM STEAM

REFORMED CHURCH, UNIONVILLE

SATURDAY, SEPT. 13, 1941

FIRST STEAM AT 4 O'CLOCK, D. S. T.

Come Bring Your Friends — Everybody Invited

TICKETS $1.35   CHILDREN UNDER 12 YEARS 60c
1.50   75

This ticket for the Unionville clam steam has obviously done duty for two years. The fall clam steams were held every year from the 1920s through 1955, when it was decided that clams had become too expensive. For the price of your ticket you got as much as you could eat of steamed clams, chicken, gravy, sweet and white potatoes, sweet corn, homemade pies, and everything else needed to make a meal.

This is a very popular destination on the Onesquethaw Creek near Dean's Bridge in Clarksville, especially for fishermen. A small cliff and waterfall are apparent in this *c.* 1953 photograph. To the right is a pool of water known as Boulder Pool because of the large rocks that never wash away. The Native American meaning of Onesquethaw (pronounced "O-nits-quat-haa") is "stony bottom," which is very obvious in this picture.

The Onesquethaw Falls near Clarksville looks much the same today as it did in this postcard from the early 1900s. Teunis Slingerland built a gristmill at the foot of the falls on the right around 1755. The path leading to the mill was too steep for wagons, so farmers had to use horses to carry the wheat and corn to the mill. The falls are about 40 feet high.

· JANUARY · 12TH, · 1899 ·

Yourself and Lady are Cordially invited to attend a

✳ BALL ✳

At Houck's Hotel, Clarksville,

Thursday Evening, January 12, 1899.

Admission to Hall, 50 Cents.

Supper, 75 Cents per Couple

Music by Jackson's Orchestra, of Albany.

Houck's Central Hotel distributed this advertisement for a ball at Houck's Hotel in Clarksville, c. 1899. Before television and motion pictures, community balls were frequently held at the local hotels. They were a popular source of entertainment and a place for young people to meet and socialize. How could you go wrong when "you and your lady" could have supper for 75¢ and then dance to a live orchestra from the city?

The Clarksville baseball team, c. 1898. Shown from left to right are (sitting) ? Reinhart, Charles Rarick, Alex Crounse, Bert VanDyke, Milton DeVoe; (standing) Balt VanAlstyne, Bob Pomeroy, Clarence Hotaling, Wallace Ingraham, Elmer Slingerland, and Nicholas B. Houck. Clarence Hotaling taught in the Stony Hill School and later became a lawyer. Note the padded uniform pants.

The Bennett Hill House near Clarksville was one of the many boardinghouses in the hilltowns in the early 1900s. It was part of a 200 acre farm that supplied its own poultry, dairy products, fruits and vegetables. The crest of Bennett Hill offered a magnificent view at an altitude of 1150 feet. At this time, c. 1920, the brochure advertised excellent roads for motoring.

What was originally called Cold Spring Cave is located in Clarksville. Frank Gregory's house stood near the entrance. One of the carved inscriptions on the cave walls among the fossils reads, "D.C. Gould Aug. 12, 1864." In 1963 it was discovered that Gregory's Cave (Cold Spring Cave) connects with Clarksville Cave (Ward's Cave). Clarksville Cave ends one half a mile away at the "pool room," which has a deep pool of water in the floor and a slit in the ceiling emitting light.

Here, the proud fisherman, Chester Hand, holds his catch for the day in front of his 1928 Chevy in Clarksville. Beyond the car is an octagonal building which was originally a bandstand. It was later used for storage by Ingraham's Garage. It has since been removed. To the right is the garage which was built by Standard Oil and operated by Johnny B. Comstock. The garage was purchased by Everett Ingraham in 1931.

Federalberg

The Helderberg Castle, also called Federalberg, was built by Bouck White on a cliff overlooking New Salem. He was an artist, writer, pottery maker, minister, and philosopher who graduated from Harvard in 1896. White began building the castle in 1934. He made pottery in the castle by a "secret" process which required no firing to glaze. His source of income was from the sale of this pottery to tourists. The castle was partially destroyed by fire in 1944.

The old Indian Ladder Road passes through the Helderberg Escarpment, c. 1900. This road follows the route of an old Native American trail once used by the tribes of the Schoharie Valley. A felled tree, lying against the cliff, enabled the Native Americans to scale the rock face, hence the name Indian Ladder. Today, stairs lead to the Indian Ladder Trail where the old road used to pass through the cliff face in the John Boyd Thacher Park.

These well-dressed tourists pose by the Indian Ladder in Thacher Park, c. 1925. This ladder is not the original, nor is it in its original location. It was built so the tourists could safely climb down in order to get to the Indian Ladder Trail. The original ladder was located where the old Indian Ladder Road was blasted through in the 1820s.

These people are camping out along the Lower Bear Path in John Boyd Thacher Park during the opening year, 1914. Emma Treadwell Thacher gave 350 acres of land in the Helderbergs to the State of New York to create a public park in memory of her husband. John Boyd Thacher Park now encompasses 2,300 acres along the Helderberg Escarpment.

These boy scouts are at the dedication accepting John Boyd Thacher Park by the State of New York on September 14, 1914. They were representing the Native Americans of the Helderbergs. Over one thousand people were present and the official speakers were greeted by the cheers of the boy scouts. From left to right are Earl Smith, Harry James, Don Taylor, and Bill Taylor.

Mine Lot Falls in Thacher Park is about 100 feet high. This has been called Mine Lot since the days of Stephen VanRensselaer, the old patroon. The pyrite found here in the yellow rock was mistaken for gold. Both Native Americans and settlers mined the pyrite for the manufacture of paint. Much of the hollowing out of the rock is not natural weathering but the result of mining.

This 1916 photograph shows some of the girls at Camp Pinnacle in the Helderberg Mountains. The girls' camp, founded by Harriet Christie and Lucy Jones, opened at this location in 1914. It has remained open to this day, although it is now co-educational. It is run by the Albany Bible Institute and is known as the Pinnacle Christian Camp and Retreat Center. The building to the right was the main building, with the auditorium to the left.

Indian Ladder Lodge, or "Osterhouts," was located above New Salem and was operated by the Osterhout brothers from the early 1930s until the late 1950s. They had an orchestra every weekend, attracting people from miles around. The large dance hall on the right burned c. 1954. During the 1940s, all three brothers and their families (13 in all) lived upstairs. The building was later sold and has since burned.

The Osterhout brothers—Wyman, DeForest (Bud), and Everett (Ebb)—stand behind the bar of their Indian Ladder Lodge, c. 1935. Note the mounted deer and fish on the wall and the old cash register. In the 1920s, their father, Thomas, had an ice cream stand across the highway (Route 85) and down the road toward New Salem.

"Under The Laurels"

THURSDAY AND FRIDAY NIGHTS
MAY 4th AND 5th, 1916

Red Men's Hall, New Salem, N. Y.

Benefit of C. E. Society of Reformed Church

CAST OF CHARACTERS.

Frank Colewood .... Edward Weidman
Kyle ("Ky") Brantford .... Millard Hallenbeck
Ike Hopper, servant .... Elwood Hallenbeck
Bob Button, servant .... Howard Winne
Zeke, servant .... Florance Bouton
Sheriff .... Rollo Sisson
Mrs. Milford .... Adelaide Albright
Rose Milford, an adopted daughter .... Florence Allen
Polly Dowler, servant .... Annabelle Young
Sooky Button, servant .... Esther Sisson
Regulators .... Willie Schermerhorn, Walter Albright

SYNOPSIS.

ACT I—The Milford Estate. The contested will. Conspiracy of Brantford and Mrs. Milford.

ACT II—The will set aside. Frank and Rose penniless. Brantford's annoying attentions to Rose. Quarrel of Frank and Brantford. The latter plots vengeance. Bob Button, the spy. Rose's humiliating situation as a menial.

ACT III—Scene 1—Meeting of the Regulators at the haunted cabin. Ike and Zeke concealed to listen. Their great danger. Scene 2—Cliffville jail. Frank under arrest. Assailed by Bob Button. Desperate encounter. Frank escapes, and soon Rose enters to release him. Button's triumph cut short by the timely arrival of Ike and Zeke. Storm scene. The flight.

ACT IV—Brantford's absolute power over the Milford family. His continued attentions to Rose. His threats to foreclose the mortgage.

ACT V—Attempted escape of Rose. Her re-capture. Brantford's triumph suddenly ended by a sheriff's posse. Happy denouement.

PLACE—Mountains of the Central South.

Curtain rises at 8:15 p. m.   Admission, 25 cents.
Ice cream served after the play.

Performed in May 1916, *Under the Laurels* was one of many plays offered at the Red Men's Hall on the North Road in New Salem. Residents recall spaghetti suppers, scout events, church plays, square dances, pool tables, and voting in this building. The building was originally a Methodist church built in 1850 and closed in 1904. The Red Men met here for many years. It is currently the home of an upholstery shop.

The first Punkintown Fair was held in 1942, sponsored by the New Salem Patriotic Association, to provide gifts for the men and women in the armed services. Following the war, the fair was continued by the newly formed fire department to raise money for the trucks and firehouse. This photograph shows the fairground on a busy weekend in the early 1950s. A favorite ride was the merry-go-round called "Old Tinkaboom." The tradition of the Punkintown Fair continues today.

Civilian and military employees of the Voorheesville Army Depot enjoy a clambake at Picard's Grove near New Salem, c. 1945. First on the right is Clara Lounsbury and eighth from the right (kneeling) is Martin Hogan. Picard's Grove was opened in 1916 and continues to be operated by the Picard family today. They are well known for their clam chowder, clambakes and lobster bakes. The farm once had apple, peach, and pear orchards also, but all were removed in 1956 because of a growing shortage of help.

By 1900, baseball had become a popular sport and many communities had a team. There was much competition between the communities. This New Salem baseball team, c. 1925, would play, among other teams, New Scotland, Clarksville, and Voorheesville. The players are, from left to right, as follows: (front row) Ed Weidman, unidentified, Wyman Osterhout, George Sadler, Elwood Hallenbeck; (back row) ? Vosburg, Harold Higgins, unidentified, Aden Crabill, and Jake Dolder.

The Indian Ladder Drive-in—located on Route 85 across from the Mount Pleasant Cemetery—used to be a popular place of entertainment. This postcard advertisement shows the movies being shown in September 1950. Movies cost 60¢, with children under 12 admitted for free. The drive-in closed in the 1970s. On at least one occasion, extra entertainment was provided by a herd of dairy cows from an adjoining farm which were loose at the drive-in. The Voorheesville Methodist Church held summer drive-in services here from 1956 to 1968.

The Fourth of July celebration at the New Scotland Presbyterian church in 1942, during WWII, was well attended. The flag over the door represents the number of New Scotland residents in the armed services at the time. Arthur Pound, a New York State historian and prominent New Scotland resident, was addressing the gathering with a patriotic speech.

A baseball team made up of Voorheesville youngsters posed for this early 1900s photograph. The team played in a field near the old foundry beyond Voorheesville Junction. Baseball was an important summer social activity for the young and old. The third boy from the left is Raymond Raynsford.

The popularity of baseball extended to Voorheesville in 1885, the year they formed their first team. Voorheesville played teams from Guilderland, Albany, and Cobleskill, as well as the local hamlets. In this *c*.1910 photograph, the third player from the left is Ray White, and the last two on the right are Jack Smith and Mike Pafunda.

The Harris House, *c*. 1900, was opened for business by Morris Harris in 1889. Famous for its clam chowder, it was the second hotel in Voorheesville. It served as a town courtroom and also a gathering place for political conventions, athletic events, and agricultural meetings. One can only wonder if these men were here for an athletic event, a convention, or a trial.

124

The Bandanna Minstrels were presented by Voorheesville Post No. 1493 of the American Legion in March 1952, at the Legion Hall. Minstrel shows were a popular form of entertainment from the late 1800s until the 1950s. The people shown in this photograph are, from left to right, as follows: (first row) Mike Michele, Ken D'Arpino, Barney Kavanaugh, Lois Alkenbrack, Dave McCartney, Lou VanAlstyne, Joan Goergan, Frank Sullivan, Patty DiScripto, Cindi Wright, Tommy Curtis, Nobel Adams, Dick Klopfer, Ken Van Alstyne, Joe D'Arpino, unidentified; (second row) Carol Brunk, Marian Schaible, Jane Schultz, Julia Fields, Mary Ricci, Aggie Tork, Barbara Sullivan, Gladys Bloomingdale, Mary Balesgen, Sadie Rzany, Phyllis Fallone, Beverly Gage; (third row) Marilyn Felgentreff, unidentified, Shirley Kammerer D'Arpino, Alice Sperbeck, Edna Ablemen, Geraldine Slabom, Jenny Sickles, Helen Cox, unidentified; (fourth row) Mickey Fields, unidentified, unidentified, Bob Slabom, George Wood, Harold Pitcher, Frank Person Jr., Gene Sickles, Ray Cox, Joe Benedict, Louis Durante, and Ralph Cox.

For several years, the Voorheesville PTA sponsored a school picnic every June, including kindergarten through grade 12. Pictured is a picnic at Murray-Jennex Park on Orchard Hill Road in 1951. A variety of games and races were offered for each grade level, along with soda, hot dogs, hamburgers, and ice cream. Each student received five free tickets to spend at the picnic.

This car belonging to Charlie Fields rolled into the pool at Windlespecht's Beech Grove in August 1938. The grove was west of the Voorheesville Elementary School off Route 85A. There was a 10¢ charge to swim. They also had a roadside stand selling hot dogs, ice cream, soda, and candy. Beech Grove opened in the 1930s and closed in 1942 because gas rationing made it difficult for people to travel there from the city.

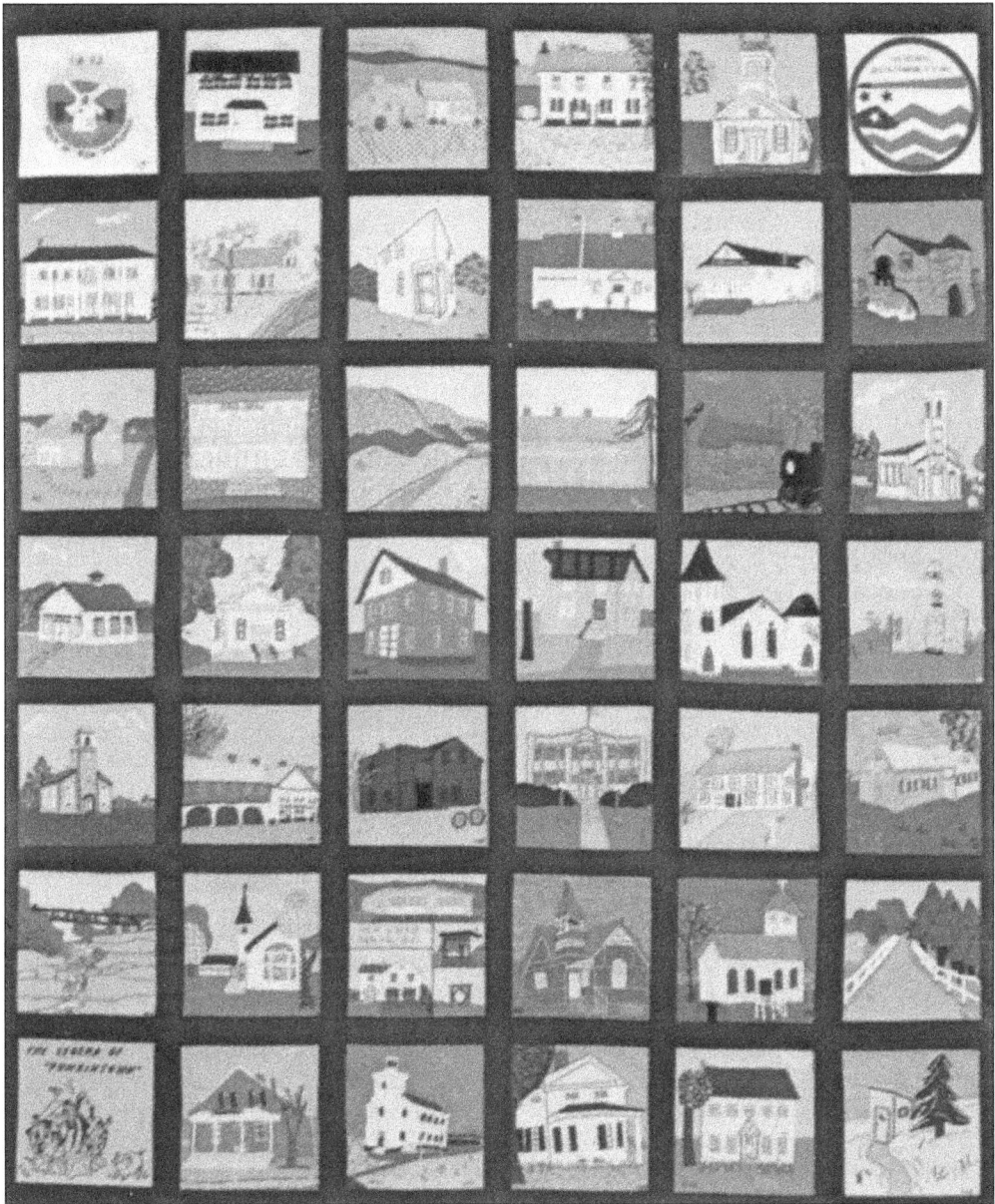

In 1976, the New Scotland Historical Association sponsored a Bicentennial Quilt project, led by Lillian Batchelder. Many women within the town appliqued squares showing historic sites in the town. The quilt top was sewn together, a quilt frame set up, and many women quilted around each square. It has been displayed at the Voorheesville Public Library and the Museum of History and Art in Albany. This quilt is currently on display at the New Scotland Historical Association Museum at the Wyman Osterhout Community Center in New Salem. It is open from June to October on Sundays, from 2:00 to 4:00 p.m. Hours are expanded in July and August to include Thursdays, from 10:00 a.m. to noon.

ACKNOWLEDGMENTS

Many of the photographs we have used are from the New Scotland Historical Association collection, some of which were gathered at Old Photo Days. Others were provided by Town Historian Robert Parmenter's collection of slides and photographs, and the photograph collections of Timothy Albright, Joseph Hogan, Martha Slingerland, and Norma Walley. Timothy Albright shared much information about Thacher Park with us. Some of the information about Voorheesville was gathered from Dennis Sullivan's book *Voorheesville, New York*. In addition, many town residents have loaned us photographs specifically for this publication and have patiently answered our many questions as we worked on this endeavor.

Among these are Ann Gephert, Sam Youmans, Allison Bennett (Former Bethlehem Town Historian), Otto Schultz, John Loucks, Frances Hoff, Gordon Tarrington, Robert Klapp, Millie McCartney, William Hotaling, Gertrude Smith, Sarita Winchell, Ann Houghtaling, the Clarksville Postmaster Janice Filkins, Marge Berenger, Doris Vanderbilt, Paul Applebee, Dorothy Wilkinson, John Lonnstrom, Peter VanZetten, Willard Osterhout, Virginia Pitcher, Lee Flanders, Betty Mason, Evelyn Berger, Michael Ricci, Wesley Jacobson, Irene Kisselberg, Clinton Wagner, Earl and Beverly MacMillen, Diane Elmendorf, Lois Wood, Thomas Coates, Janice Genovesi, Robert Shedd, Elizabeth Badgley, Robert Griffiths, and the many others who answered our calls. We would like to thank Sherry Burgoon, who proofread and edited this book for us.

We would also like to thank our very able committee, Margaret Dorgan, Joseph Hogan, Martha Slingerland, and Norma Walley, for all of the many hours spent on picture selection, research, writing and layout of the book. We have enjoyed working together to create this work for the Historical Association and hope the readers find this pictorial history of the town informative and interesting.

Finally, we would like to thank Arcadia Publishers for making it possible for us to create this publication. It has been a dream of the Historical Association to publish a book of this type for many years.

—Robert and Marion Parmenter

www.ingramcontent.com/pod-product-compliance
Lightning Source LLC
Chambersburg PA
CBHW080903100426
42812CB00007B/2144